Beat
the
Odds

Guarantee Your Retirement In the New Normal

Beat

the

Odds

Guarantee Your Retirement In the New Normal

David Reindel

with Steve Marsh

To order additional copies of this book, contact:
Xlibris LLC
1-888-795-4274
www.Xlibris.com
Orders@Xlibris.com
138056

CONTENTS

ACKNOWLEDGEMENTS

While a great deal of information in this book comes from decades of my own experience and research as an investment advisor, I would like to thank Gradient Investments, LLC, GPS Design and other noted sources for additional insights and data. From those sources and more—including the Social Security Administration—concepts involving Social Security-related financial planning were much enhanced.

Additional information came from sources garnered while composing two of my previous books, including *Don't Die Broke* and *We Survived the Crash*, which incorporate a range of sources including my radio shows and data banks from the insurance industry.

I would also like to thank my wife Janet Reindel—and our staff at Reindel Solutions—for helping me make successful retirements possible for virtually hundreds of people.

Special, heartfelt thanks go to my many loyal clients, who have followed me through the years to preserve their retirement lifestyles.

David Reindel

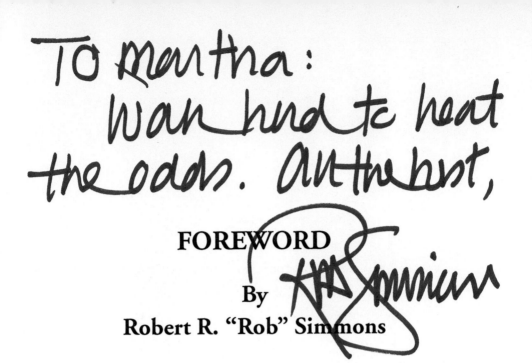

*To martha:
Wan hnd to heat
the odds. All the best,*

FOREWORD

By
Robert R. "Rob" Simmons

A little over four years ago I was invited to give a speech in Washington, DC, on the topic of "Navigating Politics in 2008." My host was Raymond James and we were staying at the prestigious Four Seasons Hotel. My job was to present the political "lay of the land" in such a fashion that the 400 Raymond James clients in the audience would be able to make sound investment decisions during what was looking like a rough year.

After running through all of the political candidates on both sides of the aisle, and making a prescient observation that Senator Barack Obama was "an articulate new voice that speaks to the issues bothering the electorate," I concluded that, "2008 will be difficult, turbulent and unpredictable."

The audience was hushed. This is not what they wanted to hear. After all, businessmen and businesswomen like certainty so that they can make long-term decisions. Uncertainty is even worse than bad news because at least with bad news you know what it is. Uncertainty is the unknown and that's really bad.

Finally, a lone voice spoke up in the rear of the room and asked a question: "So, what do you recommend?"

Almost in jest and without hesitation I responded, "Buy gold!"

Everyone in the room burst into laughter.

I tell this story because it says a lot about human nature. And it tells me why I like, and respect, David. It's really very simple. As humans we take risks but we value security. For example, I have invested in the stock market my whole life but only once did I play the slot machines in Reno, Nevada. Why? Because investments pay off—gambling does not. The casino always wins.

The second part of the equation goes back to a story my late father—an inveterate investor—told me when I took over my own stock portfolio. He said, "Investing is easy. You buy low and sell high." I was curious and asked, "But how do you know when it's low and when it's high?" Dad said, "That's the trick and you need to find trusted people who know what they're doing."

David Reindel is someone I trust and he knows what he's doing. I say that as someone who has known David and his lovely wife Janet for a decade. In addition to knowing them, I have read his previous books *Don't Die Broke* and *We Survived the Crash*. These common sense books are filled with good advice and anecdotes from everyday life. They make a lot of sense to me. Here's why:

My investing experience comes from my childhood. My father's father was a self-educated businessman with Irish roots who made a small fortune in manufacturing. When he died, he left me a small stock portfolio and by the time I was 16, I was reading the stock pages every day to see how I was doing. My dad gave me advice about what to buy and sell, and it was "fun to play the game." At one point I bought shares in Rexall (Drugs) and the stock tripled.

That was it for me. I didn't buy clothes. I didn't buy a car. I bought stocks. That was my life in high school and college. But when I was drafted by the Army and went to Vietnam, there was a challenge. I wondered who would manage my growing portfolio. I needed someone I could trust, so I chose my dad.

Years later when I was in the CIA and headed back to Vietnam, I had to make the same choice. Dad was getting older. He was retired. So I chose a family friend with a small investment advisory firm who I trusted would never sell me out or send me wrong. After all, as an investment advisor rather than a stockbroker, he only made money on commissions that were based on the size of my portfolio, rather than on trade commissions. His interest was to grow my holdings, not to "churn" them with trades. It was a good choice that works for me even today.

But here's the situation: As a younger man I always took calculated risks. My investment philosophy reflected my life choices. It was aggressive but, more often than not, paid off over the years. I remember telling Dad I was going to buy shares of Warren Buffet's Berkshire Hathaway stock at around $11,000 per share. Dad said I was "crazy" and that no stock should be sold at that price. I went ahead because I felt it was a good choice and I was really impressed by annual reports from Buffet and Charlie Munger. The growth rate of the company was exceptional. My advisor agreed and we bought a few shares. Years later, we sold it all for $77,000.

Here's the real point: That was then and THIS is now. I am no longer a young person. I am over 65, on Medicare and Social Security, and I have a pension income from my years of public service. But how do I ensure that my future will be protected? What if I get sick? What if I am disabled?

How do I "survive the crash" and ensure that I "don't die broke?"

This is where someone like David Reindel is a Godsend. He is honest. He is informed. He knows what he is doing. And he has a track record of making it work. A client of David's was quoted in one of his books. He talked about an investment David made for him, saying, ". . . If the stock market goes up, my earnings from (David's recommended) annuities will go up. And if the market goes down I don't lose everything I've gained. Mainly, I'll never lose any of my original, principal investments in the annuities."

This is a really important point. About a year ago my mother passed away at the ripe old age of 99. As the executor of her estate, I was charged with settling her affairs, and in the process, I saw that she held two different non-profit annuities—one from her college and one from a nature conservancy. Over the years, she had received a monthly check from these annuities BUT when she died they kept the principal. I have often wondered whether the purchase of one of dad's annuities would have been structured to allow the principal to go to her beloved grandchildren.

The answer is: "Yes." Dad's annuity would have passed the principal to his grandchildren.

I've since learned that having an advisor like David Reindel can make all the difference when it comes to annuities.

Which brings me to a key point in my story: It says a lot about the kind of service David and Janet provide because my 2008 prediction was filled with uncertainty. *Little did I know how much that uncertainty would grow in the coming months:* Not only did we see political tumult, the whole housing market collapsed and brought most of the economy down with it. My wife and I had worked all our lives but we watched our stock and real estate values plummet. Only quick action saved us from real disaster. Millions of other Americans were not as lucky as we were, and the economy has been dragging along ever since.

Job growth has been lackluster. Debt is piling up. Congress has not passed a real budget in four years. Medicare is in trouble and Social Security in on an unsustainable course. The list goes on.

This is not a good time to take risks.

This is a perfect time, especially for baby boomers, to re-assess where they are financially and do what they need to do to preserve their lifestyle over what we can reasonably guess would be another 25 to 30 years. I can hope I can live as long as my mom, but I wonder if I can afford it. I know I'll have to be extremely careful from now on. Back to the Raymond James speech, remember when I was asked where to invest and jokingly replied, "Gold?" Gold was selling for $535 an ounce at the time and the man who asked the question bought gold. He watched it rise to $700 and called me a few months later, asking for another "tip." I was only joking and that was the irony of the times.

David and Janet Reindel do not give "tips" and they certainly do not offer advice in jest. They are serious and they are successful. They have a plan and it works for their clients. This is why I trust them. This is also why it's important to read their books and listen to what they say.

*   *   *

Robert "Rob" Simmons served as a member of Congress from 2001-2007 and is a retired U.S. Army Colonel who has served for more than 40 years at local, state and federal levels. Prior to his congressional service, he served for ten years in the Connecticut General Assembly. After earning two Bronze Star Medals during the war in Vietnam, Rob went on to join the Central Intelligence Agency in 1969, where he served for ten years as an Operations Officer in Southeast Asia. In 1981, he was assigned to the Senate Select Committee on Intelligence and was subsequently named Staff Director of the committee, a position he held from November 1981 through February 1985. Rob graduated from Harvard University with a degree in Public Administration, where he was a Littauer Fellow, and he taught at Yale and the University of Connecticut. He currently lives in Stonington Connecticut with his wife Heidi.

INTRODUCTION

Life presents an odyssey of change as we pursue a career and build a retirement plan. When we think about the future, we hope our investments will turn our dreams into a reality that, one day, will give us financial freedom and a carefree lifestyle in retirement.

But it takes more than a dream to build a successful retirement portfolio. You need a financial road map based on a clear and solid plan. This plan must eventually include asset preservation and something more: It will include a strategy to ensure a life-long stream of income you will never outlive. To do this you will need income based on principal capable of surviving future markets and economies. Yet, the road to this kind of retirement security—your ultimate goal—can be fraught with temptation.

The road can lead to financial vulnerability based on risk, without the subsequent reward of carefree living when we need it most: during a retirement meant for fun, family time, anything but a rigorous work schedule. So, how do we get there? For one, successful retirees rarely travel alone. They find the best travel companion possible in a qualified financial expert, someone who will be there every step of the way. This person will know how to avoid hazards capable of eroding—or annihilating—your carefully mapped retirement savings plan. Your highly experienced, professional guide will also create periodic goals and milestones, all within reach of your own, specific situation until you reach the long-awaited day of your retirement with real joy—without market fears or financial worries of any kind.

I'm known nationwide for this type of professional guidance. At Reindel Solutions, with offices in Mystic, Connecticut and Warwick, Rhode Island I've been directing successful retirements based on secure income and principal for decades, and my clients have remarkable stories to share . . . . More on that in a moment.

As for retirement, some reach that special day with expectations of a carefree lifestyle. Yet, they may have unpleasant surprises in store unless their road map allows for certain financial safeguards. I specialize in this type of planning but not everyone can, especially while ensuring a certain level of increased earnings as well. My clients know from experience that I can do just that—while literally saving carefree retirement lifestyles from the ravages of any oncoming market collapse, recession, poorly placed investments and other notorious pitfalls.

Among the books I've authored in recent years—which have collectively led my readers to successful, safely protected retirements nationwide—a few of my clients talk about how I helped them provide a bedrock source of financial assurance for themselves and their families. Their stories are in my recently released book titled *We Survived the Crash*. In it, my clients tell their own stories, in their own words, which clearly illustrate a variety of investment and financial planning strategies they chose with my help. While we worked together to plan and chart those strategies, they all have one thing in common: a carefully planned foundation of financial guarantees that provide income *to this very day* no matter what goes down on Wall Street.

This is where I have been notably distinguished from many others in the field of financial services. I can work with a great variety of other professionals who have extensive expertise across the board. Yet, I've always maintained a clear vision for my clients, who include scientists, former politicians, veteran investors, you name it.

They have all come to know that I specialize in one thing, and that I do it better than anyone else in this business: I work with a complex array of stable, financial instruments designed to preserve your retirement income and principal, and—this is most important—they allow you to *be indexed in market gains*, without risk of catastrophic loss seen in recent years.

I can do this while working on all sorts of estate planning projects involving sophisticated wealth management methods. In this area, I may direct a consortium of professionals (legal, tax etc.) equally committed to your long-term success. I'm a Registered Investment Advisor, who knows how to implement a multiplicity of disciplines into my own, widely acknowledged blueprint for a safe, worry-free retirement—no matter how large or modest your estate may be.

That having been said, I can solely focus on you and your retirement plan, with results that have become legendary among those who survived the Crash of 2008, the subsequent recession and countless market downturns and corrections over the past 15 years.

For this reason, professionals from all over the financial spectrum have come to me for advice. Since the Crash of 2008 and prior market meltdowns, I have helped individual investors and corporations, clients of other financial professionals, and many hard-working people.

I have helped all of the above and more achieve greater stability and peace of mind with re-engineered strategies designed around the concept of *preservation*, while providing asset-building opportunities at the same time!

Since the crash and great recession, this kind of strategy has become the foundation of retirement planning in The New Normal and I'm counted among the pioneers. So, if you want ongoing accumulation, maximized income and/or preservation of principal, I have proven methods that have led to successful, long-term retirement goals for virtually hundreds of people.

Many people have come to me after reading my books or hearing me on the radio. My shows have aired through the years for the benefit of hundreds of thousands of people throughout southeastern Connecticut and beyond. My books have been available through the years via Amazon.com and other sources—including major publishers—and my ongoing seminars continue to be a major draw.

Yet, none of the above will ever compete with the time-honored process of face-to-face conversation. This is where I really separate myself from other financial advisors.

Given all of the above, I still specialize in a personal, one-on-one series of meetings with every one of my clients. For me, it has to be that way. I have made it a hard and fast company policy to get to know *every single one* of my clients in careful detail, *before* any financial decisions are made. From that point forward, my clients have attested *in writing* to my constant availability.

Unlike many financial professionals, including those in many large financial service organizations, I have always been quickly accessible to my clients. Whenever they have questions, concerns or merely want to talk about economic conditions related to their retirement portfolios, they will tell you one thing: I'm there for them. (This is also part of the message we put in writing in *We Survived the Crash,* and its predecessor *Don't Die Broke.*)

Personal service sounds like a simple thing unless you've endured the alternative. I've heard about the alternative from clients living coast to coast, many of whom came to me out of desperation shortly before and after the Great Recession of 2008, and they share a common complaint: When their investment chips were down and floating away, they were unable to reach their (former) advisors, who were either unable to pull them out of a drowning market or shore up their portfolios with safeguards in rough waters. Then they heard about me. Books were passed around, my professional colleagues spread the word, and my methods became known along with my expertise in the implementation of those methods.

In the New Normal since the crash, those concepts have been widely recognized but rarely mastered because they involve a great deal of study, practice and attention to detail. Using related tools, I have been able to measure investment performance with minimal to no risk exposure, offering my clients a share of market gains when the market is performing well, and an overall strategy based on solutions tailored to *achievable, lifetime-sustainable* financial goals.

Before moving on know this: Although at times my clients have called me a "miracle-worker," I want to make one thing crystal clear. I don't sell miracles. I offer time-tested solutions, solid expectations and rock-solid guarantees to back them up. Combining that with an uncommon level of direct customer service has made me one of the most successful financial practitioners in America.

CHAPTER ONE

Risk, Future Markets and You

I call it a "Season of Uncertainty."

It began with the years leading out of the Techno-boom of the late 1990s, through the tech crash of 2000-2003 and upward, downward and onward from there—until we hit bottom in '08. The Great Recession followed, defining a 10-year season of elation, fear, foreboding, momentary triumph and finally, global economic collapse.

After that, many in the financial services industry did an about-face. Formerly obsessed with trade-based accumulation, some of them turned to a more methodical version of risk management. But it's risk all the same. If risk exposure is defined as deviation from an anticipated outcome, avoidance of extreme volatility became a new focus for many advisors (although the risk-factor endured). For example, after the crash if a hot new software company deviated from tried and true product into uncertain new directions, catastrophic failures were finally counted among possible outcomes. Before the crash, too many investors had been advised to fly without a net, and many fell. But how much have we learned; are we falling into the same, risky habits?

One thing hasn't changed. To pursue the rapid gain-loss cycle on Wall Street, you must be willing to accept inevitable swings in market volatility. You must be able to afford to lose without foreseeable recovery for long periods of time. You might be more fortunate if aligned with highly skilled professionals willing to constantly monitor your individual portfolio of stocks, bonds, ETFs and the like. Unfortunately, such attention is rarely given to most investors, due to the sheer number of people willing to play on the high trapeze.

In short, to play you must be willing to pay the price. Factors including global economic markets and business cycles must be considered on a constant basis. Rapidly changing conditions demand constant re-assessment of investment valuations. And big-time liquidity is key: Will you have enough cold, hard cash to live on when you need it most, not if but *when* markets take a collective nosedive? Are you ready to lose most or all of your original principal investment? Will your net gains in, say, a family of mutual funds, perpetually outpace inflation? Would a dramatic dip in interest rates affect your lifestyle? Can you predict the outcome of global economic instability and its effect on your retirement?

If you are *entirely* caught up in the cat-and-mouse game of stock picking—either by you or someone else—or if you're riding the crest of asset allocation through a broker, you can't blame anyone but yourself when things go awry. Gain and loss goes with the territory. You stand to lose everything, or not.

Now let's change the rules. Let's reduce the odds *by removing them altogether.*

I can show you how to participate in the same game *without losing anything.* I can show you how to cruise through the hard times very nicely, adding to your principal when times are good while simply waiting out the hard times until the upside flow begins again.

Let's call my rules a method of Post-Crash Survival in The New Normal.

While others struggle to follow the old rules of volatility in order to stay aloft in the market, I offer a different set of rules. My rules are based on framing reasonable lifestyle expectations inside a dependable, measurable package of steady income, guaranteed principal and a more modest but predictable increase of that principal—while you *enjoy* life. No need to continually hover over the actions of brokers and/or the latest investment schemes. No need to let market procedures interrupt your sleep and dreams. My retirement strategy is based on little or no risk tolerance. Your risk, if you call it that, is to go for respectable earnings without risking everything for fast gains, and subsequent losses, with the latest of the hot offerings.

By the way, if after protecting your retirement with guaranteed income and principal you want to take on some market exposure, we can do that, too. All of the above is part of The New Financial Normal, but first you must anchor your lifestyle with financial guarantees.

Again, when you are ready to retire, or if you are already in retirement, one rule should override all others: Retirement is about play, not work. My retirement solutions will keep you from being forced to go back to work. It's that simple. With my tried-and-true rules of the road, you won't have to endure the gut-wrenching peaks and valleys of market turbulence while achieving your long-term financial goals.

At the same time, I can offer an intelligent way to capture gains from market investment opportunities, while minimizing volatility over multiple economic downturns. When markets tank, you won't lose a penny, but you *will* enjoy gains when markets rise again—all part of a carefree way to navigate fickle markets while maintaining your retirement planning strategy.

Much of this can be accomplished through a series of fixed income strategies, some of which are still misunderstood by many in the financial service field. Today, a variety of fixed income instruments let an insurance company take all the risk with diversified stock and bond investment programs, while you share in the gains and avoid the losses. You will enjoy a fixed income at the same time.

Another gem in my rulebook is the near-total reduction in management fees and other costs associated with equities, traditional asset allocation, and other strategies. Meanwhile, I assure a steady, dependable income and safety of principal, with many plans, including equity indexed annuities, a very respectable rate of return on your portfolio. Did you know that equity indexed annuities nearly matched or surpassed the overall performance of securities during the Season of Uncertainty, without the angst associated with market volatility through the great recession?

Well, they did, and this type of investment program is hardly a one-trick pony. My own extensive studies of financial instruments are always leading me to new and innovative features for my clients, but you can rest assured that I will always maintain a consistent policy. I favor the creation of income my clients cannot outlive, the utmost protection of principal and—should the client choose—a degree of flexibility to participate in a variety of investment options.

All of the above represent who I am—no smoke and mirrors. If your chosen advisor is like me, he will ensure ready access to himself, directly, not endlessly unanswered voice mail and staff intervention. This is because I guarantee a "carefree" retirement lifestyle, which involves direct client contact from time to time and sophisticated investment tools at my disposal to help you monitor and diversify other portions of your portfolio. It's all about contact with a real person, in my rulebook, and that person would be me.

I can help you prosper in retirement with less volatility and higher yield to achieve desired benchmarks. I would never settle for "average" results when it comes to your retirement.

The Problem with "Average"

Years ago, I discovered a great analogy called the "Flaw of Averages," a phrase I found in the *San Jose Mercury News* way back in October, 2000. It resonates as well today as it did then. It reflects the way I feel about risk when moving forward in The New Normal.

The concepts points up a well-known quote from Pliny the Elder, a Roman scholar who noted that only change itself is unchangeable, something like that. Anyone who weathered the last crash will heartily concur. Despite a dazzling array of electronic wizardry and scholarly studies outlining allegedly infallible market projections, *nothing* can be certain when it comes to Wall Street. If you have a broker and expect him or her to protect you from uncertainty, you expect too much, no matter what you've been told. The market runs on numbers and equations, yes, but it also rolls with emotion, political change, global-economic upheaval and, under certain circumstances, momentary panic due to rumors-denied and other fallacies.

Through all of the above, mathematicians have tried to come up with "average" performance tables—to help settle nerves and provide a level of market guidance. I'm a mathematician myself. I read the charts and tables. I track performance models of all kinds, from those involving insurance products to complex asset allocation formulas used to analyze securities.

The Flaw of Averages states that investment assumptions based on "average" market performance will eventually let you down. Failure to heed warnings based on the Flaw of Averages will lead many an asset manager astray, as it has in the past, leaving related portfolios vulnerable to performance-planning illustrations and other well-laid plans. Add the dazzling numbers spewing out of lightning-fast computers enabling electronic trading programs, and so-called "average" values are lost in *real-time simulations*—all the rage in both military defense planning and Wall Street investment models.

But we can't seem to evade the pesky Flaw of Averages, which is still one of the most important considerations you should make when investing in your future.

In my world, we don't deal with "averages" and other equations, we deal with hard and fast figures defining lifetime guarantees you cannot outlive. First, *you* must look at the reality of how long you could actually live in retirement. For many, this span of time will encompass 30 years or more after age 65. If you plan to live on income based on performance on the S&P 500 index, will S&P-based financial models guarantee steady income every month . . . for more than 30 years? How can S&P performance predictions truly guarantee adequate income at age 92? Following the S&P

or any other index, how can you accurately gauge a reliable rate of return? You can't. Since the S&P began in 1952, variable returns from this popular index have "averaged" around 14 percent per year, but that's only part of the picture. Placing a $200,000 principal investment into a fund and basing your annual growth expectations on 14 percent a year from the S&P, you might expect an annual withdrawal of $32,000 from your fund. You might also expect your money to last at least 20 years, give or take a few lumps and bumps in the equities market.

All I can say is this: Assume the above and you could be dead wrong.

As we have seen historically over the last few years and through the past decade, stock market volatility has been all over the board. Significant market declines and only partial recoveries have been part of the "average" norm, leaving many investors with far less principal than originally expected, also less income due to dwindling principal.

Now let's take a look at the 14 percent "average" during a 20-year period on the S&P. Beginning in 1975 with a 15.4 percent "average" return on your $200,000 investment, you would have watched the market tank within a subsequent 13-year period. Shift your starting point to 1976 and you would see the market plummet within a 10-year period. You can shift starting points and select other time periods, but the outcome will be basically the same. You would not likely experience a guaranteed rate of return, which equates to a known probability: If you assume that you would receive the projected S&P average of 14 percent for each and every year, and if you're depending on that kind of return in retirement, you will probably run out of money.

I say "probably" because lightning could strike and we could have a miraculous 20-year period in the future where annual gains remain perfectly reliable. But think about it: When, if ever, will things pan out exactly as projected? Did anyone accurately predict every downturn and correction leading up to the ultimate economic nightmare of 2008? Let's be realistic, could anyone ever come up with a truly reliable set of extrapolations designed to provide us with absolute guarantees for future markets and economies?

. . . Of course not. Regardless of future advances in technology and the perfection of physics-based market projections, you can count on the indefinite variable of human behavior to skew the results every time. And if you expect some future government to step in with a financial dream-team and create guaranteed safeguards for market investors, forget it.

Meanwhile, have scientifically based theories been applied to help safeguard retirements? To this question the answer is: Yes! Nobel laureate economist William Sharpe left a lofty job at Stanford University to devote himself to full-time research related to retirement benefits. One result of his studies was the creation of complex, simulated financial algorithms for retirement portfolios. Sharpe was surprised to find that most people in financial services were still relying on broad-based "averages" to determine the best retirement outcomes for their clients.

Guess what? They still are.

No wonder so many investment decisions went awry from the 2000 tech crash through the recession of 2008-2009 and beyond. They were based on figures distorted by a reliance on "average" market gains, which came from an entirely different time-period with a separate set of social/technological/economic factors driving markets at that point in history.

Imagine a car manufacturer trying to design a car with a guaranteed number of sales. Can you imagine car designers promising unknown sales? Take the notion a step farther and imagine a savvy board of directors approving the construction of an expensive new factory to build the "guaranteed" new car. Would they ask the design team to speculate about the needed size of the facility, in order to crank out models based on unknown demand? Suppose the design-team speculates that sales would average between 50,000 and 150,000 cars the following year. If so, an average 100,000 cars would have to roll out of that facility, a figure then fed into a spreadsheet projecting $30 million in revenues. Would the company tell its stockholders to expect dividends based on averages in this equation? No way. A prudent investor would expect less than average dividends based on a host of unknown factors skewing income projections including a potential decrease in the demand for cars, unknown future markets, or even a competitor's unexpected release of a hot new model.

Would we see "guaranteed" future auto sales in the real world? Hardly.

When the first atom bomb was being developed, simulation models were used to predict thousands of possible problems affecting production of an actual, working prototype. Scientists know better than to expect results based on averages.

Average Returns and Your Retirement

Yet, how many flawed retirement plans have been based on so-called "average" returns from the stock market? Fact is, many have been based on "average" assumptions from 10-year models seen in past decades, where a myriad of other factors created outcomes we may never see again.

Is this sort of revelation new to the financial world? Not really. Back in the 1950s, a brilliant graduate student named Harry Markowitz challenged market projections based on average market returns. Back then, contemporary investment theory tended to dote on averages. Markowitz came up with a concept eventually dubbed "modern portfolio theory," which called for the melding of *risk potential* with average outcomes. Markowitz won a Nobel Prize for his efforts and Wall Street changed forever as a result.

In spite of Markowitz' equations combining potential risk contingencies with historic outcomes, after every expert analysis was said and done, we were still unprepared for one financial debacle after the next, running from 2000 up through 2009. The 2008 crash was, in part, the composite result of markets based on investment returns, *based on returns based on speculative projections.* It has been said that many investors had erroneously been led by flash analysis from poorly rendered charts promising sky-high profits, some of those lacking foundation in fact.

Even the U.S. military began to follow ever-more precise simulation models when predicting its own future needs. Given a host of uncertainties about the broad, unknown landscape of global conflict, models and simulations are continuously used and developed in the materials-acquisition process to reduce time, resources and risk. As foreign weapons systems have increased in complexity and sophistications, our own simulation models have helped to frame future defensive systems.

Yet many in the financial world still cling to illustrations based on average returns from bygone eras.

Some such illustrations doggedly continue to support risk-immersed portfolio management for retirees, often pointing to projected outcomes based on recent market success, as opposed to long-term probabilities based on thousands of potential contingencies—*many of which pose a serious threat to your retirement income.*

In the post-crash, New Financial Normal, an increasingly savvy nation of investors is waking up to the realities of risk as we embark on the unknowns of an uncertain global economy. The nature of risk itself has become more threatening to a new generation of security-minded incoming retirees. They've already suffered from more than a few ups and downs in past markets. Now they face a future of steadily increasing market factors set to upend even the most astute and carefully calibrated expectations for risk-based immersion. This is why more and more people are looking to basic fundamentals using guaranteed numbers.

This is what retirement planning in the New Normal is all about!

Do you want to wonder what will happen, or do you want to live a wonderful life?

Given all the mathematical models used to analyze risk—and after unpleasant surprises based on the best projections possible—millions of experienced investors have returned to solid building blocks when designing their retirement plans.

CHAPTER TWO

Pyramids Don't Lie

Pyramids don't say much in terms of spewing mountains of words. They don't have to. They speak to us from the mute testament of time.

Constructed nearly 5,000 years ago, the Great Pyramid of Giza was built using more than 2.5 million blocks of chiseled limestone. All told, the materials used in the Great Pyramid could be used to build roughly 30 Empire State Buildings. No wonder it became one of the Seven Wonders of the World, yet of all those wonders, the Great Pyramid is among the last of the ancient Wonders still standing today. It could be said that this massive structure defies gravity. It remains intact at 454 feet high, nearly as high as a modern, 48-story building. It bears testament to the timeless value of solid construction on a lasting foundation based on seamless design, which has proven to be the best defense against natural elements and even time itself.

What have we learned from the builders of the Great Pyramid?

After thoroughly exploring the interior and exterior of this marvelous human creation, it could be said that the pyramid was primarily built with one, specific function in mind: to survive the millennia, to beat the odds of natural laws and survive. This was no easy task. Each stone was carefully crafted to fit into a precise design. The design was created to minimize every possibility of collapse, despite coming centuries of unknown climactic conditions.

The same kind of thinking should be applied as an integral part of your financial plan.

Look at it this way: All sorts of dazzling but fragile buildings have been erected worldwide by inventive architects. They soar to impossible heights with outer skins of sheer glass, and with inner structures built on principals of physics yet to stand the test of time. Developers today take risks to make statements. Then they move on. Does this sound familiar? How many advisors have created precariously towering financial monuments that failed to stand the test of time?

Let's get back to your post-recession retirement plan in the New Financial Normal.

Countless new computer simulations and electronic-trading models are being, and will continue to be, set up to facilitate ever-competitive modes of risk. Like the glass towers they often represent (built by tiers of risk-based investment), they have become the picture of soaring imagination. But will they stand the test of time, or will they fall to the wrecking ball in the near future?

Needless to say, we face a more complex array of financial decisions than any generation before us. As markets soar and decline, we see fewer ways to even out the roller coaster, fewer ways to invest with the kind of certainty needed to live comfortably before running out of money. It used to be that investment in a few solid American companies would secure a safe, carefree retirement. The same companies used to guarantee pensions most of us only dream about today, and old safeguards placed on U.S. trading environments have since proven inadequate. Even real estate investments and the equity in our homes let us down, underlying an all-new need to find safe, secure and predictable retirement options.

At the same time, many want to take part in rising markets. But we also know the importance of being able to lock in earnings based on fixed interest rates. Overall, we see an economic environment driving markets with less clarity and more risk, where it will be increasingly difficult to recover from financial mistakes. Add age to the equation and risk becomes all the more costly with the passage of time.

This is why it becomes vital to organize and secure our retirement assets as we age.

We must learn to place strong, dependable assets in the underlying foundations of our retirement plans. Upon those foundations we can then add other types of assets. Together, they form a strategically aligned pyramid of retirement planning, a plan I like to call the New Normal of the Post-Recession.

Asset Organization for Solid Foundations

We'll talk more about the color of money in the next few chapters, but two colors should immediately come to mind from now on, whenever you think about retirement.

"Green money" represents assets with guarantees against erosion from things like inflation, or eradication due to risk. Green money can incorporate mechanisms for growth, but this type of asset is designed to withstand the test of time, like the great pyramid. It forms a strong, solid foundation for your retirement years. It becomes the base of your financial pyramid.

Without it, you may be building towers of glass with your money, but as we have seen in years past, even the most impressive money monument can come crashing down without the strong foundation of a financial pyramid.

Next, we talk about "red money." This is money created from uncertainty. It remains uncertain because it's invested in stocks, bonds and other speculative investments lacking guarantees against the test of time.

In the coming chapters, you will discover why red money is also called "hope so" money. We hope it will perform for us. We hope it might even make us rich. Who knows?

What astute investors currently know is that Green Money is "know-so" money. We know it will be there when we need it, even after our "hope-so" is long gone, due to yet another market debacle.

We also know that both types of money can have a place in our retirement pyramid. Both can serve a purpose, so long as our "know-so" money comes first and foremost.

Hope-so and Know-so monies are basically described in the following categories: Know-so money involves income planning and legacy planning, two separate but intrinsically intertwined concepts. Know-so "income planning" calls for money coming in on a constantly reliable basis, far from the threat of stock market woes. Those of us who weathered the market between 2007 and 2009 know just how quickly the elations of mind-boggling gains can be dashed. Both up and down cycles tend to balance out one another. Ironically, the safe dependable principals behind "Know-so" financial planning have statistically equaled or exceeded the long-term gains of "Hope-so" investing. But let's get back to basics.

Know Your True Cost of Living

"Know-so" money begins with the concept of ensuring that your income will be adequate enough to provide you and your family with an acceptable standard of living. What do I mean by "acceptable?" This is where you should get together with someone who has made a career out of analyzing just that: What may be acceptable to you would be unacceptable to someone else. Why? . . . Because we have all led different lives with different levels of income during our working years.

In retirement, we must identify those things in life that mean the most to us, and ensure that we would have enough income to support them for our remaining retirement years.

Those things might include enough to travel the world, or simply to be able to travel to see friends and family members from time to time. Yet, travel may not be important at all. Some people merely want to maintain a comfortable lifestyle close to home, which would include the purchase of a new car from time to time. Others might want to work for themselves in retirement—without the angst of having to worry about basic income. Others might dream of having a comfortable home while pursuing favorite hobbies like gardening, golf, painting—you name it. We all have different ideas about the ideal retirement. Yet, I'll bet every one of us wants one thing more than any other: We want "security."

Security in Retirement Means More than Money

Of course it takes money to be secure. It would be naive to assume that we could be happy without it. Almost everything has something to do with money. Heating your home will cost money, always will. Roof repair will be a necessity at some point. Property taxes will almost certainly increase (if you can find a place where taxes won't increase, let me know), and we must prepare for out-of-pocket medical expenses given the way health insurance seems to be trending these days. Same thing goes for ensuring that your Social Security checks will keep up with inflation, which we'll deal with in coming chapters in this book.

I'll let you take it from here. Think about everything you need, everything you do, from the moment you get up in the morning. Make a list. Try to estimate daily, weekly and monthly costs of living. And if you're still working, as many would-be retirees have been since the crash, estimate what you would NOT need if retired. Would you need a constant wardrobe update, for example? Would your monthly restaurant bills be less without the recurring—sometimes habitual—business lunch? Of course not, but we all like to meet friends for lunch from time to time, so an ideal retirement would factor in some, but not all, of daily living expenses we had during our working years.

Again, it's all about our perception of absolute necessities in retirement. Some people are truly amazed after making the suggested lifestyle "list" above. Once they see what they truly need, versus what they think they need, many people are startled to discover that they are not so far from living a comfortable life in retirement.

But it means planning and commitment based on the creation of solid income, an income you cannot out live, and one based on certain guarantees that would safeguard your money. If any of the above sounds simple, look at it another way: While assessing your current lifestyle needs, it often becomes necessary to sit down with a financial professional to determine your *future* costs of living, including inflationary projections and precise expectations from guaranteed-income tools. I will introduce those tools in this book, along with outside investments you may want to liquidate in order to increase your level of guaranteed income. From there, we might even consider some kind of market investment you may want to pursue, but only after you have reached your desired goals for fixed income.

While it all sounds fairly simple, and it should, together we would take into account every source of income you currently have and how you wish to manage that income through your retirement years. If you currently enjoy hanging on the edge of your seat every day, watching for the slightest up-and-down nuance in some stock or bond fund, some people do. But would you want to plan on doing the same thing for the rest of your life? Once you have established a level of income *every retiree must have in place by age 65*, you might want to systematically decrease any remaining market risk until you reach a golden age where virtually all monies are out of risk and into income.

I have spent much of my career studying every type of income-producing investment vehicle. They tend to offer a diverse array of methods to guarantee income, either for a set period of time or for a lifetime. Some carry important features including death benefits for surviving spouses or heirs. Others offer limited levels of market participation while protecting your principal investment *and* guaranteed income.

Remember what I just said about some people preferring to maintain a foot in the market while ensuring a lifetime income that cannot be outlived? Well, you can do that while enjoying gains from the up-cycles on Wall Street. With my planning methods you won't lose a red cent during downward trends on, say, the DOW or the S&P. Yet, in this situation, you can't have it all. If you want principal and income guarantees, you'll limit full exposure to utmost market gains. But again, you avoid the possibility of market loss while allowing for frequent opportunities to grow your money—all that without the edge-of-your-seat commitment it takes to keep from losing everything, if fully immersed in market risk.

Expertise Required for Guaranteed Gains vs. Loss

Since the Great Recession of 2008, people in my profession have come to realize the necessity of securing some level of portfolio safety. That's the way it is in the New Financial Normal. From there you will encounter every sort of individual financial planner, insurance agent, stockbroker and the like. All have different ways of approaching the concept so sorely missing before the crash: safety of principal.

Let me share a few examples with you. Some professionals still favor near total exposure in the market, even for retirees. They do this through elaborately tiered mechanisms, which are still essentially linked to "asset allocation," which supposedly minimizes risk through a multi-foliate basket of diverse investments in stocks, bonds and mutual funds, even some insurance products including "variable annuities."

As for annuities, more than a few insurance agents come into the business with an understanding of basic annuity contracts and life insurance policies, but in today's market so many products come in different shapes and sizes with a myriad of different features. All told, if you line up every policy and annuity, then factor different bonus programs, fees, income features and the rest, you would find virtually hundreds of different variations on a theme.

Not every insurance salesperson will be aware of this important fact. Professional advisors, like myself, must be able to step back and start with vital information about you and your goals; then it's time to look at your existing assets and determine things like lifestyle goals based on current income—as illustrated above. Only then would I apply all relevant factors in order to align your life plan with appropriate products.

I have spent a lifetime studying and analyzing virtually everything the insurance industry has had to offer, ever since the most basic life policies were introduced, many years ago. To learn more about all that, begin with my first book, *Don't Die Broke* and delve into my pioneering background in this industry. Since those early years, and my abilities as a mathematician to move beyond "averages" into the real data behind annuities and other products, I have watched a wealth of new products come along. I know how and why they do not act alike. I know how some can be used in concert with other types of retirement planning. I can tell you how to avoid overall planning mistakes, such as under-utilizing Social Security (covered later in this book).

I can also tell you with the authority of experience that the term "financial planner" can mean many things. I, for example, am a financial planner, but I have a certain degree of securities licensing as well. Many do not. As previously mentioned, people like myself have a great deal of additional depth when it comes to understanding annuities and other insurance products. People new to the business may be aware of only a few products, for example, or products favored by only one particular carrier.

Some people calling themselves "financial planners" may favor only mutual funds, while others favor mutual funds sponsored by a narrow range of mutual fund companies, and most people know by now that mutual funds—no matter how well diversified—equate to market risk. In fact, the lion's share of mutual funds tanked under the duress of the last crash, while declining considerably before the crash during various up and down cycles between 2000 and 2009.

Still others might suggest a mix of funds—stock funds, bond funds, it doesn't matter—along with risk-mitigating insurance products such as annuities. But be careful when approaching such diverse strategies with someone who paints the financial world with a broad brush. I work with securities brokers who have the same depth of knowledge about stocks and bonds that I have about income-producing insurance products, but I work only with the best, and they tend to maintain a finely focused expertise about specific areas of the market. In short, annuities in particular have become very popular in recent years, due to their ability to protect your retirement while offering levels of increased earnings to, say, meet inflation and more.

But there are lots of annuities and life insurance policies out there, and a great many securities can be packed within a single mutual fund. It takes a licensed, well-educated and experienced professional to navigate these worlds, which is why some of the best of us work together.

At the end of the day, the New Normal demands a highly focused spotlight on the impact of guaranteed income, as it relates to any kind of investment income, including your future income from Social Security. In the coming pages you will see why Social Security is one of the best deals out there, also why you must pay careful attention when choosing the right time to start receiving your Social Security checks. When properly timed with the use of annuities and other investments, your Social Security payments can become a significant part of a great retirement.

More on that in moment, but I think you will begin to see why it all must come together under one sheltering strategy. The way you plan for your retirement—or the remaining years of your retirement if you are already retired—depends on a new set of rules, as opposed to old rules applied to your working years.

Even those still in their working years have realized a need to balance upcoming investment vehicles with a level of income planning. Since the crash, and the roller-coaster economy of the past 15 years, we have all learned the value of bedrock safety for our money.

This is why you must become passionate about your knowledge of "Know-so" versus "Hope-so" investments. You must be able to absolutely spot the difference at first glance. After reading this chapter, you should know enough to take a good look at your retirement plan and realize the need for improvement. If you have too much "hope-so" without enough "know-so," and if you fall within a critical age category, it's time to sit down with a "know-so" professional.

-For pre-retirees, it is equally important to understand the need for a balance between the two.

-For early retirees, understanding is one thing; it's critical to achieve that balance *right now*.

-For those in retirement, if you haven't already achieved the balance between "know-so" and "hope-so," it is not only a must, you should now be implementing plans to phase out of "hope-so" and cement your financial foundation on "Know-so."

As my practice has evolved, I've been able to work with a broad range of financial professionals, from those in securities to legal experts dealing with elder planning. Through it all, I still maintain what I have said throughout my other books, radio programs, newspaper and magazine interviews and public appearances nationwide: *There comes a time in most retirements when risk-taking is no longer appropriate.*

That moment will differ for many, but in my opinion the rule still holds.

I began this chapter with a discussion about building a financial pyramid. The pyramid will contain different building blocks for different people during their earning years, when some of us would be young enough to be able to afford to lose yet recover in time to retire.

If, however, you really study troublesome market declines from late 1999 through 2009, you will begin to see a pattern. Up and down cycles don't always wind up as far "up" as they were before the "down" cycle came along. Years went by before down-cycle investments recovered to original levels. During that critical time, some people aged enough to find themselves on the brink of retirement, unable to recover enough financially to rebuild their pyramid. They had to take a haircut in retirement lifestyle as a result.

Some were unable to retire at all and wound up depending on family members for support.

This is why it's so important to base your retirement pyramid with a solid foundation of "know-so" income. It becomes especially important if you want to think about legacy planning, either for a surviving spouse, adult children, grandchildren or a favorite charity or non-profit foundation.

You can't even think about the legacy planning process without it.

The all-important legacy planning process must have a strategic roadmap in place to create a separate groundwork for a second pyramid, your legacy pyramid. If properly designed, your legacy pyramid can go beyond a simple financial bequest to encompass a college education for a grandchild, or a level of income for a surviving spouse after you pass away. This is going to be important for almost everyone. While helping people of all income levels and every asset level, I have also worked with people dealing with major estates, involving complex legacy planning involving a host of issues: heirs, grandchildren, policy beneficiaries, foundations, charities, you name it. Given the array of future considerations included in complex estate planning, the tools I offer from decades of expertise are typically ideal for multi-generation strategies.

Tax Planning in the Battle of Erosion

Everything should be considered in light of tax planning, especially estates in the process of legacy planning, but taxation applies to almost everyone.

To answer one common question, yes, Social Security can be taxed, even though Franklin D. Roosevelt promised otherwise at the inception of the

Social Security program. This implies that even if Social Security will be safe, as promised, for those born in or before 1958, taxation will still be the unchangeable factor of change itself. Again, I'll discuss this in more detail shortly, but let's face it: When it comes to taxation, nothing seems to be sacred in Congress. It's only a matter of the composition of a political majority at any given time.

This is why it is so important to have something in place allowing for methods of taxation control. While none of us can control the rate of taxation, or the rules applied to the way we are taxed, we can take advantage of existing rules as they apply to a very specific array of investment options now available. While your money will be taxed at some point, we can determine whether or not it would be taxed going into, or coming out of, certain types of investment vehicles.

We'll get into IRAs and related legacies, but it's also important to know that annuities and related strategies can help mitigate the tax hit as well. You must apply the tools carefully, of course, and if you've ever made a simple mistake on your IRS form, you know what I mean. That's why you need help when dealing with certain types of annuities and other tax-advantaged instruments. I can show you how to apply them to measures legally provided in the tax code for your benefit.

When I start working with clients, it is sometimes necessary to have a look at the way previous tax years were handled. Sometimes clients have missed important ways to mitigate taxation while strengthening their financial pyramid—not only in advance of retirement but during retirement as well. As you may well imagine, this requires a high degree of knowledge. At last glance, the IRS tax code had grown beyond 71,000 pages in length, which can look like a bad thing at first but look again. Throughout this lengthy document are a great many, often-overlooked, tax rules put in place to ease your tax burden. But you have to find them. Then you have to put them to good use which often calls for specific tools to make them work.

More than once I've run across someone who missed valuable tax-saving opportunities *built into the tax code for our advantage*. Again, many financial products have evolved through the years to help you take advantage of, and manage, those opportunities.

To learn more, all you have to do is ask. Through my office, you will find people who love to pore through the 71,000-page IRS tax code (believe it or not). They love hunting down measures already in place that can benefit your specific situation. I then apply special tools to enable those measures because it's all right there, and it can make a real difference both before and after you retire.

Asset Allocation

I have always been such an advocate of guaranteed principal and lifetime income I probably haven't addressed certain concepts enough, concepts like "investment diversity" and "asset allocation". Let's take a closer look. These strategies typically involve the buying and selling of stocks, bonds, real estate investment funds and the list goes on. These instruments can be purchased individually or packaged in mutual funds, which can be layered by ranks of brilliant financial managers and computer models to help reduce market risk.

Somewhere in between all the equations and assurances of maximized earning and the like, Wall Street practitioners often ask clients to determine their own risk tolerance versus growth expectations. This is because people often hope for the moon, profit-wise, while demanding safety for the money they make in the market.

Safety and the moon are difficult to put together, especially since the crash and previous market declines during the past 15-year period.

Since the crash, and during the long slog through the depths of the recent recession, the term "asset allocation" has come to mean something more for millions of edgy investors. We've been able to watch the S&P soar to historic levels, while bonds have risen to precarious heights; however, both are subject to market risk. Bonds in particular have faced near-bankrupt municipalities and potential default. Many crash-hardened investors also know that historic market levels can reach a bursting point before a precipitous fall.

My point? "Asset allocation" now has an expanded definition. Many brokers, financial planners and other investment professionals have discovered the value of protecting client portfolios from catastrophic loss, allocating safety measures, if you will. Many do this today through the use of foundation building blocks including instruments that guarantee principal and income. What I mean is this: While too many portfolios consisted of pure market risk before the crash, many now try to incorporate a cornerstone of diversity from certain types of annuities and life insurance products.

That's where I come in. On a weekly basis, I get calls from brokers, attorneys, tax experts and other financial professionals seeking cornerstone investments for their clients. As some clients cash in liquidity for growth, many set aside a certain amount of principal to grow inside things like equity index annuities, which take advantage of limited market earnings made by insurance companies, which can invest and absorb risk without passing the risk on to their contract/policy holders. For some people and since the crash, these and other instruments have become part of an expanded definition of "asset allocation." If someone feels driven to a certain degree of market risk—a younger investor, perhaps—why not balance the impulse with future income guarantees in annuities? In this way, he can take advantage of the latest money management platforms, while negating risk with a balanced portion of income guaranteed to help mitigate volatility.

This is why you will hear me talk about Green Money and Red Money throughout this book. Even the more daring investors have come to see the critical value of "Know-so." By shoring up their portfolios with "Green Money," they have assets they can count on when "Red Money" goes up in smoke.

Certain types of annuities represent "Green Money," which can counterbalance a younger investor's calculated gamble in options—which may have more upside potential but few guarantees other than exposure to volatility.

CHAPTER THREE

Asset Preservation with Legacy Planning

You can't take it with you. This certainty takes us to the topic of legacy planning and the way it will affect your portfolio after you die. Some people plan to spend all of their assets while they live, and this may appear to be the only option for some people. After all, this is why we work hard to ensure that people will have enough money to live comfortably for the rest of their lives. That's always first on my mind: YOU and your life, unless you direct otherwise.

Then what? You would be surprised by the volume of assets most people leave behind. Even those living very frugally in retirement often fail to spend every last dime, especially if they pass away unexpectedly.

Without legacy planning, many people leave a trail of assets to probate, from life insurance policies to rental properties, boats, jewelry, and the list goes on. The consequences can be costly and emotionally draining for a surviving spouse and family members—draining indeed; assets can trickle away due to court fees and unwelcome contests during a prolonged probate process.

So, legacy planning should be considered an important process for all of us, even if our only surviving assets would be, say, a car and coin collection. If you want to die interstate and leave it all to whomever, that is your right and completely up to you.

For the rest of us, legacy planning will ultimately determine a potentially infinite range of issues, such as how much we would be able to leave for our heirs and beneficiaries, including future generations of grandchildren and, in some cases, even their children. College educations typically enter the picture during the process of legacy planning but a number of other considerations come to the table, including the creation of philanthropic foundations, trusts for surviving children/grandchildren, trusts for a surviving spouse and the list goes on.

Legacy planning is a very broad topic, often requiring my expertise along with those on my team of legacy experts. Some of these highly specialized experts may include Elder Law attorneys, tax specialists and others. If, for example, an estate's legacy plan requires the creation of trusts for specific purposes, I have the tools and resources to make sure your legacy-planning goals are implemented according to your wishes when the time comes.

Well in advance, and as part of the legacy planning process, I would carefully review where you already are in terms of your retirement lifestyle—again, to ensure that you have enough guaranteed income to enjoy a comfortable retirement. That said and done, we can look at a variety of ways to leave assets to future generations, for example, while ensuring that a surviving spouse and chosen beneficiaries would be first in line, according to your wishes.

Obviously, to make sure your legacy is in place—come what may—we should attend to key issues right away. Essential steps must lay the groundwork for a legacy plan that can be both flexible and secure for after you are gone. Let's face it, life is already short but unforeseen events can suddenly leave your beneficiaries in limbo. Too many families delay their legacy planning until it's too late, until that unforeseen event takes an important breadwinner out of the picture. Then we're left with a mess of improperly executed wills and other documents, including assets that become very important to your survivors after you die. These might include annuity contracts, burial policies, pension documents and other items essential to ensure the well-being of your survivors.

A legacy can go beyond a simple financial bequest. If thoughtfully designed, it can even instill your own values in those of generations to come: For example, you could provide stipulations with your legacy that heirs and beneficiaries of certain assets adhere to safe retirement planning involving guaranteed income and principal. After all, YOU have seen it all if you're reading this book. You've witnessed the short-term elation of those caught up in risky day trading, only to watch them lose it all in a subsequent down-cycle. You have seen the so-called market corrections and adjustments, the roller coaster ups and downs of portfolio-robbing market events, which come and go outside of truly catastrophic events like major recessions.

Since the great recession of 2008, which I discussed in detail in my last book, *We Survived the Crash*, the topic of Wealth Planning and the instruments needed to make it happen have become important to all sorts of people—not just those with great wealth.

I can remember the day I first entered a bank vault. I wanted to make sure our important papers would be secure no matter what and the inside of the vault was impressive. Dozens of safe deposit boxes lined the walls, proving that I wasn't the only one involved in this part of legacy planning. If you know me from my other books, you know I'm a car buff. Vehicle titles would obviously be important documents to someone like me, especially if the title is somehow misplaced. A lost title could put a survivor through laborious weeks of title recovery. Along with those, mortgage documents and property titles are absolutely essential to keep in a safe, secure place, like a safe deposit box locked up securely in a bank vault. Countless other information could be stored in a safe-deposit box including information about your bank accounts, insurance policies, annuities and wills.

In fact, if you haven't yet taken the time to assemble all of your important papers in a well-organized place, now is the time to start. Again, this is one area where a great many of us fail to perform. We may put it all together at one point in our lives, but as time moves on, we add documents which become scattered among too many file cabinets and computer hard-drives. Some documents need periodic updating and others just get lost, making it difficult to impossible for survivors to assemble needed information in a timely manner, after you pass away.

So, legacy planning is more than just stating our intentions in a written will, passing money along to heirs in designated bank accounts and the rest. It includes a comprehensive approach to everything from documentation to careful consideration of how assets would be passed along and preserved.

Asset preservation after your death can be an additionally tricky issue for your heirs and beneficiaries. For example, important steps must be taken to ensure that taxation will not rob loved ones of the money you intended to leave behind. Maybe you intend to leave cash behind in a bank account for your beneficiaries, but those assets could be vulnerable to unnecessary taxation. If beneficiaries lack adequate access to those funds, or if individuals in the bank are there to sell various investments to your heirs, when they show up to withdraw assets, your friends and loved ones could be exposed to predatory, inexperienced salespeople out to pocket a tidy profit for themselves—through the sale of poorly performing instruments to your heirs.

Without proper legacy planning, all sorts of subtle traps await your loved ones after you pass away. Think about it: All it would take is for a young, inexperienced heir to inherit a substantial amount of lump-sum cash. If exposed to the wrong people, your heir's entire legacy could vanish, virtually overnight. Some people are easily persuaded to invest in the worst kinds of things—especially when they suddenly receive a bucket of money, and especially if they are elderly or very young.

The value of legacy planning is not unlike the value of planning for your own, carefree retirement. "Peace of mind" can be difficult to attain without assurances that your money will be properly and safely distributed, according to your wishes, after you pass on. It's that simple. But it's not so simple. Graduate business programs in top universities are dealing with legacy planning with more fervency than ever before. Family wealth planning is no longer limited to rich and famous people. Everyone is getting into the act—to the point that costly trust services are being marketed to people who don't need them. This is happening all over the Internet, through magazines, and direct-mail campaigns.

But the most important seeds of legacy planning begin at home.

Facing a great reduction in Social Security income after the death of a spouse, I have heard of grateful survivors who found an unknown insurance policy, which had been sitting for years in a drawer at home. Then, we need to think about scattered Social Security documents. We'll talk about reductions in Social Security in coming chapters, and how to prepare surviving spouses with supplemental income. But for now, try to think of all of the above as an integrated process that must be systematically planned, with proper instruments in place to assure the best outcome for a virtual "wealth" of reasons.

The wealth would be yours. After you die, your wealth—whether a few thousand dollars or a few million—could be easily wiped out by predatory investment schemes, inflation, taxation and sheer, misguided generosity. Here, I mean beneficiaries being influenced friends and family members who may appear with hands out, trying to persuade a kindly surviving spouse to share the wealth—to the detriment of the spouse's livelihood in future years.

Meanwhile "back at the ranch," one of the worst things to leave behind is a disorganized drawer or two of family financial documents, some of which allude to missing documents misplaced between the house and the bank, or things arbitrarily assigned or left in the hands of various family members or friends—who may be deceased or estranged. This can leave heaps of tedious paper work and unnecessary legwork for your surviving beneficiaries. So, if you have any doubt whatsoever about being able to instantly locate things like insurance policies, bonds, securities, cash, gold or other assets—including property titles, et cetera—it is time to clear the air, clear out the family "money drawer" and get it all in order.

When you do, you will likely find things that no longer work to your best advantage—*while you are alive.* Expired insurance policies may need replacement. Existing policies may call for a change in beneficiaries. The potential found in a family "money drawer" is often rife with opportunity for improvement (or loss if certain matters are left unattended).

In some cases, you may want to take a stack of neglected assets and bank accounts—some earning less than 1 percent these days—and consolidate them into a new generation of secure instruments, which could be earning 5 percent or more without risk of market loss. Updated instruments can do all that and provide your surviving beneficiaries with *guaranteed income for life.* Consider this, while putting your legacy in order, you might very well discover untended assets that would improve your own lifestyle while you are still living.

These days, there are various ways to secure documents without having to keep them in a safe deposit box. Create a virtual online "vault," where you can go anytime to review its contents without having to go to the bank. In this way, you can have a complete picture of your financial picture, and your legacy, at your fingertips. All told, having this kind of organization in place will—in itself—help protect your heirs and beneficiaries from exposure to risk after you're gone.

As I've said through the years, when I sit down with my clients, I take a good, comprehensive look at their objectives. From there, we examine everything available to create the strongest, most beneficial planning strategy for their individual needs.

So much of the time it's not about the money, it's about knowing precisely what the money will do. It's about knowing that we have "green" money to count on, both for ourselves and for our heirs.

This is why it is so important for us to get together and create a new kind of vault. It will be there for the secure management of your assets and for your legacy. It will be put in a place where you and your designated beneficiaries will be able to find it immediately.

Ask yourself if you have all of the following: powers of attorney (including properly executed medical powers of attorney), wills including living wills if necessary, also trusts, insurance policies, annuity contracts, investments including bond and securities documents, tax returns, important family mementos, property deeds, vehicle titles, gold/precious gems, and other items.

Make a list. Begin the assembly process right now. It may take time because certain documents (like birth certificates) may have to be obtained from government agencies, before they can be used in, say, the Medicaid application process. After that, meet with your financial planner and devise the safest, most accessible way for you and your designated beneficiaries to view the vault. Given a world of electronic tools at our disposal these days, information about much or all of your assets and legacy could be made available to you, 24-hours a day, in a safe, secure environment.

You will never again play hide-and-seek with your financial information. After we create a financial snapshot of your retirement, and your legacy plan, it will be available anytime. We can include a detailed record of your assets, reports from me and my staff, and the rest of your legacy team, along with financial suggestions I would pass along from time to time. In this way, our meetings would be more fruitful when we get together.

This kind of process points to another important difference between me and other people in my business. More than anything else, more than the safe and secure retirements I create, more than the way I target surprising solutions to help people *retire right now*—rather than wait around for dead or risky investments to perform—people have come to me for years for the personal, one-on-one service I provide. Among the huge brokerage houses and franchised financial planning services popping up all over America, I have become something of a vanishing breed.

I am well known for picking up the phone when my clients call. They know they can speak to me when they need important information, or when they simply want to chat. I have never deferred client contact to a staff of people trained to defer difficult questions. Also, if I decide to take on a new client, we tend to meet face-to-face on a regular basis because this is not only important to you, it's important to me. This is why I have been successful. I have learned as a mathematician to efficiently allot my time to important matters, including client meetings, and in my rulebook important matters focus on meeting with my clients whenever possible.

Through me, you will be able to access and manage your assets and income from a central location. You will receive important updates about your asset and legacy plans, and you will have access to my team of professionals, who come to me for my expertise as I send my clients to them for plan-integrated issues related to taxation, legal matters and the rest.

Through me you'll have a personal team of professionals available and working year-around to protect your interests as *you* decide to have them implemented. In my office, we're a close-knit team and we're dedicated to protecting your carefully designed plans, from retirement living to your chosen legacy.

Your Legacy Plan Defines *You*

Legacy planning is a comprehensive process to be implemented once your retirement strategy is in place. This is because wealth preservation can lay the foundation for the integrity and substance of generations to come, people who will remember you and carry on your name. But legacy planning also has a life-changing effect on you when you are alive.

Because people know you have planned not only for yourself but have put a special plan in place for them, let's face it, people will be more inclined to celebrate your life while you are living. You also stand to gain an enhanced level of communication with your beneficiaries. You will be able to have an effect on how they think, how they approach their aspirations and how they move forward in their own lives. In the end, the actions of your children and grandchildren would be more likely to reflect who *you* are, which can be more important as we age and look back at the life we have lived.

I haven't talked much about heritage, but we all have something to be proud of, some kind ethic we would like to instill in those we leave behind. I came up with wonderful parents but like many people in this country, I wasn't from a wealthy family. We didn't have much money at times, although we had a lot of love and that's a kind of wealth you cannot buy. That's one thing I want to convey before I go, also the fact that I have always had to work hard. I learned to love work at an early age. I had to make my own way much of the time, and I learned the joy of living through the zeal for working and making enough money, which made it possible for me to help others later in life. I hope that will be part of my legacy, among many other things.

I donate a good deal of money to charities that help everyone from autistic kids to needy families, and I get involved myself. I went into detail about all that in my first book, *Don't Die Broke*. But it all comes down to one thing: Planning your legacy will say volumes about who you are while you are alive. It can lead to new friendships and alliances. It can change not only your heart but your life for richer, more fulfilled quality of living. In short, it can add greatly to the enjoyment you have during the best years of your life—your carefree years in retirement.

One part of my legacy will hopefully promote the need for hard-working perseverance, and the notion that anyone can do almost anything if they buckle down and get at it. The next part involves sharing the wealth, once we have it, in ways that will change how people think, therefore how they live. That's the way I personally think about the effects of legacy planning. I've always said that, at some point, it's no longer "about the money"—it's about how we feel about ourselves, and the friendships we've formed, both inside and outside the family.

Getting down to the business of leaving your legacy, we all pursue the best means possible to plan for retirement, but few of us look at legacies until we near the last nine yards. We often fail to plan when it comes to passing assets along, but think of the opportunities if we do it right. Do your legacy planning in advance and, if you wish, you'll be able to share the "why" of your plan with your heirs. You can also make changes more easily in an existing plan, while you are alive.

In the New Normal and on behalf of their survivors, more people are transforming their accumulated earnings into insurance products like annuities and life insurance policies. This is where legacy planning comes in. You must properly structure your assets to assure that they will go to your beneficiaries according to your intentions.

We have talked about tax planning and we'll return to that subject elsewhere in this book. I consider prudent tax planning very important for legacy planning as well. Almost nothing hurts more, after all the grieving comes and goes, than for a surviving beneficiary to pick up a big tax bill you might unintentionally leave behind. As one alternative, certain types of annuities allow money to grow tax deferred, but you need a planner like me to help ensure against mistakes that could lead to serious, tax-related legacy issues you might unwittingly leave behind for your beneficiaries. You might want to "stretch" money to be left behind, for example, to provide for people yet to be born—children of your children, or even children of their children. We all have different goals. We want to avoid leaving money to unintended beneficiaries, of course—I'll leave that to your imagination—but whatever your intentions may be, don't wait until you're too sick to take care of your legacy business. Call someone like me right away so we can review your plan and make adjustments accordingly.

As outlined in this chapter, details abound in legacy planning and I have much to share, but a significant portion can only be covered in face-to-face meetings. One thing I will tell you right now is this: If you're not sure if your intended legacy plan is in order, it probably isn't.

The following issues will help you better understand what you need to do:

- *Have you taken current control of your assets by reviewing your plan within, say, the past year?*
- *Are any of your retirement funds at risk? (If so, they're at risk for surviving beneficiaries.)*
- *Do you have too many balls in the air, account-wise? (If you can't recite the location of each account, you might think about strategic ways to consolidate them.)*
- *Have you planned your tax deductions after distributions kick in?*
- *Are you taking your currently required distributions? (We'll cover this one, later on.)*
- *How often do you update your list of beneficiaries?*
- *Have you set up ways to stretch future distributions for your beneficiaries? Call me.*
- *Have you adequately planned how you wish to take your distributions? Things change.*
- *Are you planning to establish separate accounts for your beneficiaries?*

If you're still wondering why you should bother with any of the above, picture your own situation with the following story in mind: Auto racer Dale Earnhardt Sr., was very successful in the racing business, but even more important to Dale as he aged—even more important than all the trophies—was his real creation: Dale Earnhardt Inc. It was a highly successful company and a legacy he had planned to leave for his heirs. In the process of planning his estate—or not—Dale Senior left the company to his new wife, naming her as the owner/operator of Dale Earnhardt Inc.

His son from a previous marriage, Dale Earnhardt Jr., was the star driver for the company and a high-profile performer in the racing world.

But two people in the company never quite got along. In fact, they were reportedly at odds with one another from the beginning, and the net effect from this dysfunctional family dynamic was the eventual destruction of Dale Earnhardt Inc. Before Dale Sr. died, he was the ointment in the gears that alleviated friction in the family. But when he was gone, the company began to run like an engine lacking oil in the crankcase. We all know what happens to an engine without oil. They don't run far, do they?

If you plan to pass ownership of a family-owned company to one or more beneficiaries, who will own, manage and/or simply benefit from company operations?

In the quiet of your own meetings with appropriate professionals, these are issues to be resolved for the future harmony of your family or other designated heirs. As you can see, when it comes to legacy planning we're just touching the iceberg—we haven't even seen the tip!

And when it comes to money, have you established separate accounts for your beneficiaries?

I have been helping families organize their retirement accounts into manageable, reliable assets, which not only guarantee lifetime streams of income, they can also be arranged to secure legacies as well. Don't wait. This is a critical part of an overall, carefree retirement plan, and we can put it all together *right now.*

CHAPTER FOUR

Planning for a Rich, Full Life in Retirement

So far, we've said a lot about the nature of risk. We've cut to the chase about ways to mitigate loss through creation of income, and other aspects of prudent planning. But let's take a look at the fundamental mindset needed to put it all together and keep things going in the right direction.

When we're young—and enjoying the bustling energy of our earning years—we tend to place a major emphasis on staying afloat in the workplace. We're caught-up with performance, doing our best. We want to succeed and climb up the latter in the best way possible. We want to increase our income and live life to its fullest, raise a family, perhaps, and explore every option to maximize our lifestyle while we work.

But let's face it. We don't worry too much about saving. In fact, many of us don't save at all. Or, we save very little while accumulating the trappings of better lifestyles: better cars, bigger homes, and greater learning opportunities for our kids including college. Some of us save through company investment plans although many of those are changing rapidly—traditional pensions are a thing of the past in many a work place; the traditional company

401(k) has sometimes proven suspect in recent years depending on the level of management expertise.

Under current economic conditions at this writing, things are looking up and market returns look good, but an unsettling under-current has changed the way many of us look at the market—no matter how momentarily successful it may seem. We now look much more deeply than we used to. More of us are concerned about the effect of global economies and market investments, and we're asking questions:

- Are stocks backed by adequate assets in a particular company?
- Is the stock market too high to justify the bedrock beneath it?
- Are bonds running the risk of overheating since the crash?
- Are global economies going to affect the U.S. in a significant way? (China, for example, could decide to reduce further investment in our national debt, as its own real estate markets implode from under-performing assets.)

And so forth. From here on, economists indicate that an ever-integrated global economy will create ever-more volatile markets.

What does this really mean to individual investors simply hoping to retire when the time comes, without having to work? There WILL come a time when we will no longer be able to work. Many of us are in denial about it, but eventually our services will no longer be required in the workplace. As a group, we may be rendered obsolete by age. Employers will demand younger workers less prone to illness and capable of higher output. It's a fact and it's risky to think otherwise in the New Normal.

Here's the flip-side of the equation: At the same time, we are expected to live longer and longer, due to advances in medical science, easier living conditions, better nutrition and healthier lifestyles. Will all of the above make us more marketable in the workplace as we age? Probably not. As we progress into the future, we're watching technology replace multiple workers with one or two, who handle machinery capable of doing many tasks at once. Since the crash of 2008, employers have discovered that fewer office employees can handle multiple tasks once performed by many more people. Profits may increase accordingly, along with a decrease in the number of workers on the job, but the bygone Industrial Revolution at the turn of the 19th century did the same thing.

Today, companies are consolidating operations at a seemingly ferocious rate in order to ensure survival of the company. If they made it through the last crash, they've learned not to dismiss the possibility of another economic tumble in the future. As investors, so have we. Individuals are far more sensitive to market risk and economic uncertainty than we once were. We're a more astute group of risk-wary investors than we ever were, and that's a fact.

As a Registered Investment Advisor of many years, I've noticed a dramatic change in people working up to retirement. I've noticed the same thing in people entering or already in retirement. At one time, it took much longer to explain how annuities work and why they're so important as tools designed to minimize market volatility and risk.

Since the crash, more people have come to understand the importance of annuities in retirement planning. Despite heavy advertising and promotion of risk-immersion in market volatility, more people understand the real "value" of annuities. They "get it." Annuities preserve principal and create income, but they also accumulate market-proof earnings: "Value."

Instead of wondering about the value of annuities, in the New Normal people want more specifics about a new generation of, say, "equity index annuities," which allow contract holders to share a portion of market earnings through investments made by the annuity carrier—without risk of losing their previous gains or their principal investment. Now they look for the best, latest bonus programs and features. At the same time, they look for annuities from the strongest companies with high ratings.

And they look for a new world of income features.

What used to be a somewhat exclusive world, relegated to people savvy enough to grasp the vital importance of secure principal and income, we now have a more diverse environment. Annuities are becoming more sophisticated and more competitive, while life insurance products try to offer certain benefits traditionally included in annuities. At the bottom line, income guarantees are more important than ever to more and more people nearing, or already in, retirement.

What does it say about us as a group, in the New Normal, after going through the rigors of a post-chaotic recession and global economic meltdown?

It says we're saving more, spending less, as we near retirement.

But then I still have to deal with people in denial. They act as if nothing ever happened. They see Wall Street soar, forgetting about the past. But I can still promise the same, eventual outcome of risk and market volatility: Regardless of the way the market performs, it will do so at roughly the same, long-term rate it always has, which in the past decade ran at about the same rate as annuity earnings over a ten-year period.

Here's the problem: Some people still avoid thinking about financial matters from a long-term perspective. They fail to consider real numbers based on maximized probabilities of life expectancies. They fail to look at hard numbers and real research. They avoid making valid estimations based on mathematical analysis of the figures. They fail to estimate just how much they would really need if they live longer than expected. They fail to *plan* when it comes to ensuring that their money will last until they die.

I was working on my first book, *Don't Die Broke*, well before the crash of 2008. In it, I predicted problems for people without guaranteed assets and the book came out, ironically, as the recession hit. Investors caught in the meltdown say the book was prophetic.

With equal irony, I can now say that many have gradually slipped into old habits. Once again, they are vastly underestimating the amount of retirement money they will need. Instead, we're seeing indications of investors falling into the same old trap. After suffering big losses in the recent meltdown, they try to pour more money into risk in order to recover what they've lost—and hope, against all hope, that they will recover and surpass their last financial high-water mark. In this way, they hope to make enough money from the stock market to retire.

This might work well-enough when we're young, with a good many working years in front of us. Pass a certain age with the old "lose-and-recover" mentality and you find yourself past the age of 50, hoping a winning lottery ticket will sort it all out.

It says too many of us are again risking more and saving less, and what I'm saying is this: If you are over the age of 55, in my opinion you absolutely must be *risking less and saving more.* If you can adopt this philosophy at an even younger age, you will succeed in retirement—again, this concept is based on my own experience, mathematical probability and solid *proof* from the retirement outcomes of my clients.

At present, it looks like we're finally beginning to recover economically. Real estate has finally bottomed out and is rising in some areas. The market is at a near all-time high and *banks are showing signs of more liberal lending practices.*

The overall financial environment in this country is not entirely unlike the early years leading up to the last recession. The DOW recently achieved near-historic highs.

This is precisely the time to come in, sit down with somebody like me, and get serious about setting some workable, realistic long-term retirement goals. Forget about "Hope-so" now. Get on the "Know-so" train before it leaves the station . . . again.

Let's begin with a realistically achievable milestone strategy. This strategy would incorporate assets you already have in place and the rate of savings you can set aside. From there, we would choose instruments that would provide the right amount of income you will need—along with maximized Social Security planning—to assure a comfortable retirement lifestyle. I have found that once people understand how the plan will work for them, they will energetically pursue a savings regimen to achieve success.

So much of this is about attitude, as seen in sports and other areas of achievement. Once we clearly understand what it takes to achieve a clearly identified goal—once we KNOW it will work when we get there—it's much easier to get that winning attitude. The importance of saving overpowers the need to spend. Retirement becomes more important than momentary status symbols. We learn to relish what we keep, rather than what we throw away on baubles.

When people have the winning attitude, they tend to move with amazing speed to reach their retirement goals. Once they understand exactly how much they will have to spend *each month* in retirement, for the *rest of their lives,* saving will become the game to win.

Understanding this basic, motivational principal, we then address the moment when it becomes necessary to phase out risk-based investment in favor of savings-oriented instruments designed to guarantee a lifetime income *you cannot outlive.*

Managing Our Own Retirement

Here's the truth: In the old days, companies spent lots of time and money both managing employee retirement plans, or pensions, and paying into their employee plans with matching funds and the rest. They spent lots of money hiring the best fund managers to maximize gains for employee retirement plans. But that was *then.*

Now many companies no longer offer pensions. They no longer maintain the level of investment expertise they once had. They no longer offer the same level of retirement plan contributions they once did.

In the New Financial Normal, it's up to *you* to manage your own future in retirement. Unless you're one of the lucky ones in a company still offering fat retirement pensions and the like, you know what I mean. But here's the good news: Together, you and I can pick up the slack and we can *do just as well, even better, and you will have 100-percent control of your money.*

One thing I forgot to mention about the "good-old days:" If your company went under, or you were laid off, you were out of luck. Your retirement plan was like a train frozen in time on its own track. You had to pick up with a new company and start over. But the real 800-pound gorilla in the room was a declining level of management and administration. We had less access to information about our plan performance. We saw less flexibility and a disturbing trend, especially during the ten-year period before '08. We saw declining 401(k) performance.

If you were reading popular consumer-finance magazines of the day, like *Money* magazine, for example, you probably noticed that more people were rolling over their IRAs into more diversified plans they could control. They did this with the help of financial planners working with computer models to create "asset allocation" strategies, which would supposedly layer more or less 100 percent market risk to minimize loss in down markets.

The move was logical enough. Companies were offering less in terms of financial management service and administrative access. Fees were high, returns were less than what people thought they could expect with a more independent financial planner. They went with the conventional wisdom of the day: diversified risk through packaged mutual funds. But nobody was really saving. Instruments set up to preserve assets—like annuities—were often overlooked in a frenzy to maximize gains with risk.

The rest is history. Many were maximizing risk until the day they retired. Many were still in risk in retirement. Many of those people had to find ways to go back to work. As many of the same people soon discovered, former jobs or commensurate levels of income were no longer available due to age factors, skill sets and other hurdles.

But the rules are different in the New Normal. Many save to retire with guarantees because they know that if they don't, they run the risk of repeating a historic lesson we would rather forget. My advice: Remember the history lesson of the last crash and be prepared.

In today's New Normal, we know to plan on living longer while having to manage our own retirement funds. Many will base retirement planning on the "flaw of averages" rather than accepting the fact that *more than 50 percent of us* will live longer than expected. They still can't understand the risk of outliving money we save while working, and the risk is even greater for women.

Savings vs. Life-Expectancy Check List

To prepare for the realities in this chapter ask the following:

- **Are you prepared to live into your late 80s, or well into your 90s?**
- **As you get older, who will manage your retirement assets?**
- **Will you have a qualified manager in place if you become incapacitated?**
- **Will you have a plan that can guarantee a fixed source of income you cannot outlive?**
- **If you are a woman, will you have a different plan than one designed for men?**

- **Have you planned to maximize your Social Security with offsetting strategies?**
- **Will your plan account for inflation?**
- **Have you considered the effects of taxation on income vehicles when they mature?**
- **If you are over 55, are you investing less than you are saving for lifetime income?**

Perhaps you have considered all of the above. If so, it's time for a tune-up to make sure your plan incorporates instruments designed for maximum income guarantees, inflation, tax planning and your maximum life expectancy.

If your current plan lacks any of the above, you are not in synch with retirement planning in the New Normal. If so, my best advice is to find a financial professional who understands the necessity of everything on this list. Then sit down with me, or a like-minded planner, and implement the principles above. Make sure you will have enough income to survive the future, no matter what happens. With that accomplished, if you wish to pursue other types of investments, I can help.

Meanwhile, please remember the following and avoid hard lessons of the past: Save More, Risk Less, and Plan on Living Longer than You Currently Expect to Live.

CHAPTER FIVE

Income & Retirement *Guaranteed*

Let's move into some of the latest New Normal strategies. These involve retirement plans with certain guarantees. I'm not talking about "if and when" concepts but a plan you can count on. As mentioned in the last chapter, I've discovered that when people are given a practical goal they *know* they can reach, given a method that they *know* will be workable, they are more likely to go after that goal with a winning attitude.

In other words, a light goes on when we understand how to beat the odds of average expectations based on probability tables on Wall Street and the ups and downs of market risk. This applied years ago and through the crash of 2008, and it applies now. In fact, it applies now more than ever, and I'll tell you why: Today's market is based on today's economy, which is based on a different set of rules than we faced back in, say, 2000. Today, we're in a sort of homogenized global economy. More factors will affect our retirement portfolios going into the next decade than ever before.

This is why we have to be ready to convert at-risk "maybe" money with funds directed at failsafe guarantees. Part of the New Normal since the '08 crash is the fact that many more planners are on board with this concept than ever before, but more products and options are out there, all of which offer a complex array of outcomes for your money in retirement.

All of a sudden, everybody wants in on the act, including a host of planners just beginning to get their feet wet in the world of guaranteed income and principal. I've been solidly in it from the beginning. In fact, I was there in the early days when life insurance essentially came in one, plain-vanilla package—look for more on that in *Don't Die Broke*.

Before moving on to the "must-haves" of New Normal retirement planning, let's begin with the following essentials. If you aren't ready to deal with the realities of this list, you aren't ready to deal with protecting your retirement. Fortunately, many of us have already dealt with some of the items below, but not all, so let's take a look.

Ten Common Mistakes in Estate Planning

1.) **Putting Off the Inevitable.** Otherwise known as "procrastination," this is probably the most common culprit leading to potential disaster when it comes to your estate. If you won't put a well-organized plan into place for the preservation of everything you own, who will? Answers abound including: the state in which you reside, former acquaintances and associates who have little or no connection to your family, utter strangers who look to probate notices for easy money.

2.) **Failure to organize important documents and store them where others can find them.** Ask almost any caregiver who has gone through the death of an elderly family member. They will likely say the worst part of the ordeal came after the funeral, when family members had to sort out a chaotic drawer-full of important documents, requiring the location of other documents—power of attorney, etc.—in order to settle matters with the estate, pay off pending utility bills, etc. Consider the time required to plan a desired distribution of assets after you pass away; now imagine all that time going out the window because no one can find the proper documents.

3.) **Avoiding Estate Planning Assuming *"It's Reserved for the Wealthy."*** First, the term "estate" applies to everything you own. That's all it means and your estate may be far more sizeable than you think. Once you begin to tally up bank accounts, vehicles, furniture, art, electronic devices, stocks to mutual funds and insurance policies, among a myriad of other items, you may find yourself holding a significant "estate." Look at it this way: How much of everything you own would you like to tote out to the sidewalk and leave for scavengers? Without some form of estate planning, you might as well do just that because your surviving spouse, friends, children and grandchildren may have to fight for your assets.

4.) **Failing to review and update your beneficiaries.** Have you gone through a divorce? Would you like to have your "ex" come into a windfall from a life policy you forgot to update? Did your daughter and beneficiary marry a "pen pal" who happened to be sitting in prison at the time, before your daughter passed away unexpectedly? How would you like your surviving spouse to face your former son-in-law-on-parole in court over contested distribution of your home and furniture, after you were deemed incompetent and sent to a nursing home, where you passed away?

5.) **Failing to plan for taxation.** When you begin distribution of your IRAs and other instruments, tax issues may arise, which could leave you with a hefty tab from the IRS. Other assets may face similar consequences, but with careful planning, you can find numerous avenues out there to minimize, or eliminate taxes. This could apply to inheritance and gift taxation, along with other issues tied to your estate. Estate tax penalties can be avoided if you sit down with a financial professional and review your options.

6.) **Lack of "gift" planning.** Numerous strategies allow you to reduce gift taxes, which kick in above annual gifts of more than $13,000 per individual, or $26,000 per couple. If you want to contribute to a child's education, for example, annual gifts could spread over a period of years. Strategies could involve different methods known to financial professionals, including the creation of certain trusts that utilize various investment vehicles.

7.) **Assets Jointly Titled.** Jointly titled assets can run the gamut from bank accounts and real estate to investment vehicles of all kinds. In the event of the death of a spouse, this practice may come in handy to avoid probate. On the downside, jointly held assets become an issue in the event of divorce. Creditors may attack assets of a joint account holder and joint account holders can misappropriate assets, so it takes careful consideration when jointly titling assets.

8.) **Leaving everything to your spouse.** By leaving all of your assets to your surviving spouse, you may sacrifice the spouse's share of an estate-tax credit offered by the U.S. government. It is important to review the latest rules applied to estate tax credits, which have changed periodically through the years. Also, certain types of trusts and investment vehicles can help with estate tax planning.

9.) **Assets naming your estate as beneficiary.** This can trigger an ongoing nightmare for your surviving beneficiaries. When you name your estate as beneficiary of your assets "pursuant to the terms of your will," you have just condemned to probate what would have otherwise escaped the probate process. The result will be costly and time consuming for your surviving family members.

10.) **Do-it-yourself estate planning.** You can't imagine the level of turmoil people have left behind by using legal forms from the Internet. Assets improperly placed into trusts, or trusts wrongly applied to certain situations, often lead to problems for beneficiaries. The same level of mayhem can affect Medicaid planning, tax planning and a host of other issues. Please, take some time with a financial/legal professional before moving forward with any form of estate planning, especially in the area of wills. You may spend a little money on fees, but you stand to save untold assets when it's time to retire.

Some of you are already there: You have gone through this list time and again. You have dealt with every issue above, and more. If this sounds like you, you're definitely ready to come in and talk to me. If you haven't yet covered everything above, I can help you tie up loose ends and get your estate in order for the next phase—and, by the way, if you haven't covered all the bases you are not alone. Many people already in or nearing retirement haven't addressed every little thing.

That's what we're here for—to help you move forward and avoid critical mistakes without finding out the hard way later on, if problems arise.

As we all know, some fairly dramatic changes are set to begin when we near retirement and, for many, it can be a time of emotional upheaval. It might be a most traumatic time of life for some people because they face a major change in lifestyle. Think about it. No more set hours to be someplace with a familiar set of tasks to perform. We'll be out of the old social loop of working friends and after-hour activities. Yet, we will have all the time in the world to pursue the things we most enjoy—a big dream for many people. But not everyone looks at an endless expanse of free time the same way.

In retirement, we're way beyond marriage and the birth of our children, who have typically grown up to start families of their own, which may create a whole new array of urgent need for some retirees—not so much for others. What I'm saying is that preparing for retirement can be just as individually challenging as our individual personalities. We may *think* we have everything in common with close friends until we really get down to the nitty-gritty of retirement planning. We look at lifestyles as differently as the way we view financial security itself. Some of us may have large, extended families, with family members at the ready to help support us through our retirement years. Some people may have children or grandchildren still in need of help with education and other matters. We will all face different states of wellness. Health-care planning can be a major issue in itself, calling for supplemental health care policies or specialized instruments in place to help with Medicaid planning and a host of other issues.

For most of us, until we really get into the detailed components of retirement planning it all seems like a pending voyage into the sunset, like a permanent vacation. It will be if we act in advance to put things in order. It won't be if we defer major planning issues until it's too late.

One of the things I like to do with a new client is to sit down and get to know everything about their current lifestyle. How much do you spend going to and from work? What do you spend each week on groceries and other basics of daily living? Do you have health issues, medications, mobility limitations or someone with those issues under your care? Do you lead an active or sedentary lifestyle? Does the "meaning of life" mean lots of travel, energetic exercise or outdoor sports? When it comes down to your own personal lifestyle, the list typically keeps growing with associated costs of living growing right along with it.

In the end, we hope to come up with a list of expenses that we'll actually need in retirement: utilities, insurance, and the rest. When people finally look at the list of necessities, reality sinks in: This is what life will look like in retirement, and for some people this is one of the more unsettling moments in retirement planning, but don't panic. We're just getting started.

If you are ready to retire, you've probably been careful about managing your budget and you have achieved some level of financial comfort. After all other living costs and taxes have come and gone, you were able to save something for yourself and your retirement years. Then the day finally comes when you walk away from work. The next day begins without the usual preparations for work, including a long slog through morning rush hour. You made it. You're retired.

Not everyone will reach this joyous moment. Not everyone will be able to set aside hurdles ahead in retirement. Some will feel the need to compromise their own lifestyle to help grandchildren with college expenses. Some would have put it all behind them, including a home mortgage now paid off.

But everyone faces one reality. We'll finally become spenders, not savers. No more paychecks; instead we'll begin to draw on our savings. Will you be ready to manage your own finances?

Be Your Own Manager

I don't mean you'll have to manage everything. Many people have some sort of financial expert looking after their finances in retirement. Many have teams of financial professionals on hand—people ready to handle whatever comes along. They won't have to break stride in the pursuit of happiness.

Yet, we still have to take some responsibility. We have to manage our lives to a certain degree, even while working with financial professionals.

For one, your lifestyle will change in retirement and you will be the one to manage the change.

Two, your savings will definitely be affected. You will either have to tap into your savings in retirement—not a good thing if you can avoid it—or you should be able to use your savings to create income, without risking your principle.

Three, you must re-think your attitude about risk. For some people this will be the toughest hurdle of all. Some people thrive on the adrenalin high of risk during their working years. Even though constant market setbacks, downturns, corrections and recessions have stripped away large amounts of assets (and future income opportunities), some people think risk is the only way to get ahead. It becomes addictive.

So, I'll say it again: You cannot sustain a risk-oriented approach to retirement and expect your money to last as long as you live. This is an oxymoron. The two concepts do not go together. To sleep at night during our retirement years, we must adjust our risk-orientation to allow for a cornerstone foundation of financial guarantees. Ask any retiree who went through the last crash and recent recession. This is a given. This knowledge is part of the New Normal in modern-day retirement.

As the list above suggests, you must start implementing real changes NOW if you haven't already. As President Dwight D. Eisenhower once said, "Plans are nothing; planning is everything."

Working Reality

This can be hard for some people to accept, but part of the adjustment we need to make is to see the end of our *ability* to work. A disturbing number of people haven't saved a dime when they reach retirement age. Others might have saved but lost all their retirement savings in the stock market. Nearly four in ten people will be forced to retire early due to poor health, which will trigger a variety of necessities covered in coming chapters related to Social Security.

Regardless of the circumstances leading to retirement, many people think they will be able to continue to work until they drop, but reality says otherwise.

Forced into retirement for a variety of reasons, many will find that in the New Normal age will play an important factor in employment sustainability. As previously noted, companies have learned to downsize and fill their ranks with younger workers earning less. They often work in demanding situations once handled by more than one worker. Older workers may not even be considered for such job descriptions. Older workers already in place may be laid-off without replacements under forced attrition policies among companies leveraging profit against employment costs. If you are laid-off at age 58, after devoting a working life to narrowly focused work-place skills, what now? Without a ready market for potentially outmoded skills, you would be forced to retire, unless you could quickly rebound through available job training programs. Some companies offer re-training programs but in the New Normal economy since the last recession, many don't. Employee attrition due to outmoded skill sets will be one of many factors facing the long-term unemployed. Given another economic downturn, the whole cycle could begin again . . . and again.

A surprising number of people have meanwhile been forced into retirement to care for others, including ailing family members. One spouse may be forced to stay at home to care for a sick parent while the other spouse continues to work. The loss of income thus becomes a burden with unforeseen consequences and retirement planning can be affected.

All I'm trying to say is that people in their late 40s, 50s and early 60s should consider the above and start planning NOW. If you want to learn about the most proactive strategies to plan for forced retirement, come in and talk to me. Hopefully, we'll have enough time to plan a normal entry into retirement, which tends to call for more manageable changes in lifestyle.

Managing Changes in Lifestyle

We all want to envision retirement in the best way possible: visiting friends and relatives, spending more time at the beach or on the golf course, or spending more time together. That's part of the goal in retirement planning. But it's not the whole picture. You also must plan for the unexpected, which can throw the best-laid plans for a nasty loop. Retirement plans can unravel if a spouse is in an accident—an accident not adequately covered by insurance to handle gap fees and expenses—but this is just one of many surprises we would include in a solid retirement plan. We also might look at the eventual likelihood of a nursing home stay and how to cover family members, in order to avoid watching retirement savings erode.

Inflation has been a factor in retirement planning—not recently but in decades past—and economists have long predicted a re-birth of significant inflation. Here, I can offer a variety of solutions designed to keep your retirement income on track—without it being sidetracked by an unexpected surge in inflation. In fact, inflation and taxation are two of the most commonly overlooked factors in retirement lifestyle management, but these hidden traps can be addressed before you enter retirement.

Inflation, taxation, unexpected illness and more: All contribute to a need for flexibility through an adaptable retirement plan. As we near or enter retirement, it is essential to ensure a steady, dependable stream of income, to guarantee principal and to plan for emergencies. All of this can be accomplished through a wide array of features offered by insurance products, alone.

Note the use of the term "insurance."

Risk and Your Retirement

During our younger earning years, many of us had a cavalier attitude about investing. Saving wasn't really part of the picture. People were caught up in acting on stock tips, or letting their retirement account ride with some unknown manager hired by their employer. We had steady income to count on and plenty of time to recover from unexpected drops in the S&P. We could ride out the ups and downs of the market. But as we age, we lose the luxury of time. I've already said this and I can't say it enough so let me put it another way: During later years in the workplace, if we lose 20 percent in the market, the new reality is that we might have lost 20 percent of our future income *for the duration of our retirement years*. Yet, even in our mid to late fifties and beyond, some of us keep thinking that if we lose 20 percent, we will get it all back in the next market up-cycle. Sure, it's possible, but if you recover just enough to get back where you started, would the recovery make you "whole" again? Unfortunately, the answer is, "No." A variety of factors including fees require an average recovery of 25 percent to put you back on Square One. If, for example, your $100,000 account lost 20 percent in a given year, a 20 percent recovery would return your account balance to, say, $96,000.

To try to make up the difference, some advisors suggest that investors create an account set-aside to fill the gap, in order to put their savings back on track, which is fine while you're working. When you're not, you stand to run into real problems as a retiree trying to recover from market losses.

Understanding the dynamics of retirement should lead to a dramatic shift in attitude when it comes to risk versus income. Continue along the old risk-and-return course of investment planning and your savings would be affected. For many, savings would be severely affected by a market correction . . . for life. That's the point. Major market set backs are no longer momentary in retirement. They have an effect on monies available to sustain guaranteed income. Get to the sustained-income factor too late in your retirement and you stand to run into serious problems.

This where people automatically think about Social Security and how it might cover gaps created by unforeseen events. In retirement, employment checks stop and unemployment checks begin, but the reality is plain to see: Any additional income must come from you and without the old source of income from employment. So, you have two choices: You can try to manage extra income by yourself, through investments that may become increasingly difficult to predict; or you can set up a steady stream of income through a structured investment vehicle.

While it may sound simple to create a steady stream of income from a lump-sum investment, complications abound. Some investments require a steady hand. You must re-visit some investments on a regular basis to watch for hidden fees and expenses, especially as the market goes through the usual rise-and-fall cycles requiring shifts in investment strategies. This can occur in mutual funds, for example, and the fees can mount rather quickly, so with mutual funds you would need to gauge in advance how much income you would need to withdraw in order to maintain your lifestyle, without eroding principle as you deal with inflation, taxation and other factors.

Does this sound like a retirement strategy you can count on?

In the New Normal, since the crash of 2008 and well before that fateful time in history, astute investors learned to demand real guarantees before entering retirement. At a time when we would rather be out with friends on the golf course, we surely don't want to be strapped to a laptop in the clubhouse, nervously watching our investments rise and fall. And there's the tip-off: Some people are stuck with this kind of anxiety in retirement and you know who they are. They're the ones in the clubhouse—after a round of golf—checking market returns on their laptops. They live on improvised returns and live dangerously, in my opinion, because improvised investment strategies sometimes lead to force withdrawals of principal.

Withdrawals of principal can lead to exhausted savings in a short period of time.

Inflation

We've addressed risk and improvised income versus steady income, but before moving on to solutions we should look more closely at inflation.

Inflation has been fairly minimal in recent years but those who have lived through inflationary cycles will tell you how damaging it can be, both to income during our working years and to retirement plans.

Inflation is a fact of life. It will be with us—if not now, very shortly—and it must be considered when designing any retirement plan. During our working years, pay increases make up for increased inflation and keep us current with the cost of living. But it's important to note that we lose that advantage when we retire. As seen in previous chapters, maintaining a retirement strategy based in risk not only leaves us with an improvised approach to income, it may not account for inflation. Market losses not fully recovered certainly can't keep pace with inflation. As we move into retirement, such strategies require us to manage our own assets—which can become a game of survival as opposed to simple inflation planning.

Few people have the investment skills to manage income that would keep up with inflation.

But fear not, I have numerous methods that plan for inflation while providing steady income and—in some cases—increased income, which we'll deal with in the next chapter. For now, I'll just be blunt: Anyone promising inflation protection through market risk is simply not being realistic. In order to plan for inflation, certain income guarantees must be set and maintained. Guaranteed income must be achieved without requiring you to manage your own retirement accounts. The best way to have a safe, carefree retirement lifestyle, is to create a solid source of guaranteed income. Period.

Let's look at ways to reach that goal.

CHAPTER SIX

Solutions for the New Normal

By now you should be wondering just how to maintain a steady income in retirement that will keep up with inflation while providing solid guarantees against erosion of your retirement savings. You want to live a comfortable lifestyle to which you have become accustomed, and you want to prevent a market catastrophe from keeping you off the golf course when the stock market goes haywire.

So, how do we address the realities of retirement, future economies and the need for lifetime income?

I have spent years of careful research to address this topic, and I have studied mathematical probabilities, market-to-income averages and all sorts of concepts proposed by the insurance industry to achieve income without risk. If the problem was an easy one to solve, everyone would be doing it the right way, but too many people have stepped into the sudden epiphany of the "annuity solution" without fully understanding annuities.

The second part of the puzzle is to realize how important adept Social Security management can be. I have studied data across the board from

Wall Street earnings to insurance returns and I have found few instruments as dependably fruitful as Social Security—if, and only if, you plan for Social Security to fully maximize the benefits you have coming (most people never do).

Back to the problem of income, you are not the first person who ever grappled with the issue and you won't be the last. The solution lies with a variety of both traditional and fairly new and innovative annuity products. These are the only vehicles out there with both earnings guarantees to keep pace with inflation and the assurance of income guarantees you cannot outlive. They provide safe harbor for your retirement savings and they provide invaluable protection against the very real perils of another collapse on Wall Street—if not wider failures based on weakened economies overseas.

With certain annuities—note that I say "certain" annuities—you have at your disposal a kind of perpetual motion machine. They are almost self-managed, in a way, in that you let the insurance company do the investing. In other words, you let the insurance company assume all the risk and that's the key to a carefree retirement. In return, you settle for a respectable percentage of return on what the insurance company may gain in the market.

The kinds of annuities I'm talking about have guarantees that allow you to keep the gains you would make in a good market, without having to give them up in a bad market. In turn, these gains can be added to your principal as you live on income distributions guaranteed by the annuity contract. Not all, but some, annuities provide that you would be able to maintain that income stream for the rest of your life.

These annuities are not to be confused with "variable annuities," which act like securities in an annuity wrapper; you can lose principal with variable annuities but I'll talk about that later. I don't often use variable annuities, myself. I deal in guaranteed retirement lifestyles, and those are offered by increasing numbers of financial service companies interested in creating solid retirement plans fit for retirees.

Many of you have already heard of "fixed" annuities by now. While I do deal in that general category of annuity, the fixed annuity has gone through a major overhaul in the past five or ten-year period. Today, they can be structured to take advantage of growth and structured income for a period of time, or they can provide an income for life that cannot be outlived.

Like other annuities, fixed *indexed* annuities offer a fixed rate of return and other advantages, including tax deferred growth, etc., but unlike other annuities, they are typically aligned with the performance of a given market index, rather than offering more modest growth from interest at a rate periodically declared by an insurance company.

A variable annuity, by contrast, will not protect your principal investment and will rise and fall in value, depending on market conditions.

While a fixed *indexed* annuity will ensure the safety of your principal while protecting your past gains, indexed annuities rarely carry fees that would be deducted from your account, as seen with mutual funds and variables. In fact, variable annuities often charge additional fees when a client account decreases in value, and additional fees could be added to your variable annuity if you purchase optional riders to go with your account. Variable annuities can also carry added fees for mortality rates, expense risks and charges for administrative services.

All told, such fees can spiral up to 1.4 percent or more per year.

Certain sub-accounts lying within variable annuities can add additional fees, typically up to 1 percent per year. And with a variable annuity, adding income riders and death benefits can easily trigger additional fees of more than 4 percent annually. So, you can see how quickly fees and charges can accumulate with variable annuities.

No such fees occur with fixed indexed annuities.

On the other hand, all things have their place for certain needs. Liquid accounts are maintained in banks (earning practically zero interest these days) to pay bills and handle short-term needs for emergency cash and other expenses. Life insurance policies are great for providing lump-sum payouts to beneficiaries. Health insurance and gap coverage policies may be desirable to cover health care costs.

The ultimate role of an "income annuity" is to provide a dependable source of income, which can be set up with a degree of flexibility: Income can be taken from an annuity right away, or the annuity can begin to distribute income at a specifically designated point in the future. For example, if annuity holders want to delay taking income, a provision called a "roll-up" can do just that, but again, the income annuity's primary mission is to create ongoing income in retirement.

Also note that annuities can be applied to various Social Security income strategies, which can play a valuable role in maximizing your paychecks from the Social Security Administration. Either way, the word is finally out and growing like wildfire: Fixed indexed annuities have performed quite well against even the best risk-based strategies during periods of gain and loss on Wall Street.

Research was conducted by The Advantage Group for a five-year period between September 30, 1998 and September 30, 2003, a periodically turbulent time on Wall Street and the S&P 500. It's interesting to note that the study focused on very early fixed indexed annuities—there were only 14 available at the time—and the study also included interest credited from those annuities during the same time frame. During the study period, fixed indexed annuities that reset each year reported an overall average of 35.67 percent interest, which gave annuity owners an impressive 7 percent return per year.

Market observers will recall that the late 1990s marked a heyday for amateur day-traders feeding the market based on poorly backed securities, which in turn helped to create a catastrophic decline on the S&P, followed by an even more pronounced downturn based on notoriously flimsy technology stocks. The stock market collapsed virtually overnight, reducing some stock portfolios by 70 percent or more—not unlike similar drops in 2008 and 2009. Annuities meanwhile held firm for their investors, steadily climbing to not only keep pace with overall market returns but to surpass market gains in 2007.

In short, from 1998 to 2003, retirees in stocks lost large amounts of money. People in fixed indexed annuities maintained their principal and earnings accrued to that point, while maintaining a steady income from their annuities. While returns on fixed indexed annuities remained flat while the rest of the market collapsed, they began to rise again when the rest of the market finally began to recover after 2003.

My point: THAT was when fixed indexed annuities were in their infancy. Today's fixed indexed annuity has progressed into an instrument with all sorts of options including bonus programs and additional features—all of which have become extremely popular since the crash of '08 (for obvious reasons).

Back then I knew the value of fixed annuities and the power of fixed indexed annuities. From a mathematical standpoint, based on intensively detailed probability studies throughout the previous 50 years on the DOW and S&P, I knew that the fixed indexed annuity would become the most viable alternative to market volatility. But I had no idea just how crucial this powerful instrument would become in future years, when issues like mortgage lending policies would go haywire, along with global markets and economies few of us would ever hear expect . . . until after the crash of 2008-2009.

For this reason, we have seen a meteoric rise in the popularity of fixed indexed annuities in recent years, even as the DOW, S&P and bond markets continue to rise (to hazardous levels, in my opinion). Despite tantalizing market gains, savvy individual investors now know that in many corners of the market, the game is rigged. They know that solid retirement portfolios absolutely must have a cornerstone of safe, reliable income and principal . . . guaranteed.

Defining an era of "self-control"

We fondly remember "Granddad's pension" and the world that made it possible, but things were different back then. Company employees often stayed on for life, until it was time to retire at 65 or so. After that, employees could retire with comfortable guaranteed incomes and the income plan was called a "pension." Today's worker retires, of course, but the outcome is far different. As previously noted, traditional pensions are becoming a thing of the past but the need for guaranteed income has never been greater. It not only takes a special company to keep an employee on the payroll until 65, it takes a special company to manage the employee's retirement income plan.

Fewer and fewer companies are fully managing employee retirement plans than ever before, giving more workers control over their own retirement outcomes. This is where financial planning has entered the picture. As employees retire with less guidance, retirement planning has become more varied, more complex, with global realities requiring increasingly critical solutions to traditional pension-style retirement portfolios.

Given market performance over the past 10-year period and even before that point, people working toward retirement have become increasingly skeptical about the outcome of qualified plans like IRAs and 401(k)s. In recent years, it seemed as if traditional qualified plans took a beating nearly as often as individual stocks, even though fund managers tried to layer investments inside the plan to ease the brunt of volatility. As more workers began to see the value of their IRAs and 401(k)s slip away, many began to seek outside assistance.

There are several situations allowing for IRAs and 401(k)s to be rolled into annuities, and this has happened with greater frequency. After multiple downturns from 2000 to 2009, a new generation of annuity products made it possible to re-produce the dependability of the traditional pension. But the pension-like plan based on the modern annuity has greater flexibility and new features traditional pensioners never enjoyed. I live in a region where large companies have long relied on government contracts, which have provided careers for thousands of families around eastern Connecticut. But lately, the government has been forced to pull back on funding. The result has been a steady decline in company involvement when it comes to internally managed retirement plans. Not surprisingly, many people have hit the streets, looking for an alternative.

When people come to my office today, they sometime appear under stress of imminent layoffs and company downsizing. But even more have come to me because company structured retirement management is rapidly becoming a thing of the past. Fortunately, my industry has recognized the need to ease the burden. With my occasional involvement as a consultant, insurance carriers have created more options and features to enhance a guaranteed income stream.

People are turning to this kind of planning because they know how bad it can be when left to face the market alone. They also know about the reality of a market controlled by analysts investing through e-trading programs, which make it harder for individuals to succeed without taking considerable risk. A guaranteed income stream through an insurance company has accordingly created a comfort level of financial security for retirees, who now enjoy a significant reduction of fees and charges in the New Normal of annuity planning.

This has created an all-new call for me. Because I have an excellent reputation, also well-received books, radio shows and public speaking schedules nationwide, company managers have been calling me in to speak to their employees. In every case, when I present to a packed house of workers they are surprised to discover that retirement savings in company-sponsored plans are not locked in but easily transferable to an individual annuity, which can be of the employee's own choosing. But that's where the simplicity ends and the fun begins. Because I've been around since the early days of fixed indexed annuities, I can talk about the history of changes that have come along. I can explain why surrender charges for one annuity can differ vastly from another annuity. I can show why earnings increase with certain types of indexed annuities, and how annuities in general can work like a pension plan with greater flexibility.

I can also talk about the way various annuities are structured in a way that few financial professionals understand—especially those new to the business. Even more important is the fact that annuities are not only complex instruments, we now have a wide array of options to choose from, so it has become increasingly important for financial people to take the time to sit down and fully detail the needs of each and every client. This cannot be accomplished in a single meeting.

The years have taught me that it may take several meetings before I feel comfortable enough to make recommendations, but by then my client knows that I have taken every precaution to cover the bases. By then, I've thoroughly exhausted every possible option to fulfill my client's retirement goals—within practical, achievable guidelines.

Let me give you an example. I had a client come in the other day with $100,000. He wanted to transfer the money out of a company plan and he'd heard from a friend that I could do things his company managers would never be able to accomplish. My client wanted to keep working, but he was near enough to retirement for his $100,000 to begin providing income by the day he planned to retire. In this case, he wanted to retire at 65. He was 55 at the time. By placing the $100,000 into an annuity contract with a 7 percent income rider, he is now assured of having $196,715 in his income account when he turns 65.

At 65, he will have a steady guarantee of $11,803 every year coming out of that annuity, assuming a 6 percent rate of payout. But here's the most important part: He will have that $11,803 income for *the rest of his life.* Do the math. How can $11,803 per year last into his upper 80s or 90s? How can it last for 30 years and come out even for the insurance company? It can't, but insurance companies have deep pockets and actuarial tables to make it work.

To have the same income from cash savings, my client would have to put more than $350,000 into the bank, and then he would be dealing with inflation and other factors.

This is why I can say with a fair amount of certainty that only Social Security and this particular annuity can come close to such an important outcome, guaranteed, and with no risk exposure to principal.

I have mathematical tables on hand to show you how it all fits together, but that's the short course. Now imagine what you can do with $500,000 tied up in a typical 401(k), which may currently carry full risk exposure in the market. When I walk into a company and tell people that—with absolute certainty—I can guarantee them more than $50,000 a year from the same 401(k) with no strings or risk attached, they're often pleasantly surprised. Then they do the math with Social Security strategies I'm about to disclose in the next chapter and, Voila! They can see a nice retirement up ahead. At that point they get excited.

As I said earlier, when people get a clear, dependable picture of what they can expect, they really get involved in putting more away for retirement. Some get so jazzed about saving, old spending habits fly out the window and before you know it they come into my office talking about early retirement.

Out of the Company, Into Your Pocket: How Roll-ups Work

For those anxious to make things happen today, I have ways to turn your at-risk IRA/401(k) into guaranteed income *tomorrow.* This involves a type of income annuity that includes something called "roll-up value". Simply put, this annuity can increase the value made available to generate your lifetime income. In other words, it can increase income every year you allow it to grow—until you begin taking income. Remember what I said about annuities with built-in features that help keep pace with inflation? This one can do that and more. This annuity will continue to grow until you start taking income, *no matter what happens to the market.*

Imagine watching another market crash, safe in the knowledge that your annuity value is still growing, and that it will continue to grow until you decide to start taking income. This is another instrument that can be a powerful ally for Social Security income planning, and, like Social Security, this type of instrument provides a lifetime income stream. By contract, it will provide an income you cannot outlive, guaranteed.

No wonder the income-generation of fixed index annuities has become so popular for retirees. This innovative instrument has accordingly become one of the most sought-after tools for protecting both principal and income. If you would like to have one protect your retirement, let's talk. This might just be the thing for you.

CHAPTER SEVEN

The Secret Life of Fixed Indexed Annuities

Through all the moments of crisis on Wall Street and throughout the world, I became so enthusiastic about fixed indexed annuities I made it my mission to educate the world about these powerful instruments. While my other books talk about the fixed indexed annuity in action, I haven't really delved into the internal workings of this versatile tool . . . until now. To truly understand how it works, you should know about the following:

Basics of Indexing

First, the fixed indexed annuity is essentially a contract between you and an insurance company. Unlike some other types of annuities, the fixed indexed annuity is connected to a market index commonly available to other investors. These "indices" include the DOW, the S&P 500 and others, where securities are bought and sold.

Before the fixed indexed annuity came along, standard fixed annuities required a lump sum investment from the annuity holder, and the insurance company set a rate of interest for the annuity, which was "fixed" like a savings account, but without the shifting interest rates you see from a savings account at a bank. Fixed annuities would accordingly accrue interest for a time at a fixed rate and the account value would eventually be distributed, which worked fine for many.

But others wanted more. They wanted the rock solid dependability of a fixed annuity, which guarantees principal, among other features. Yet, they wanted some level of market participation, without having to risk losing everything previously gained—along with their principal investment. Safety with gains locked in and no risk? Sounds demanding, but insurance companies got to work and came up with something beside the variable annuity (again, with variables think of a mutual fund packaged with certain features of an annuity).

If the market linked to the indexed annuity goes up, the annuity holder receives a share of the earnings garnered by the insurance company. If the market goes into a tailspin, as millions of market investors exposed to risk lose wads of money, the fixed indexed annuity owner losses *nothing*. The insurance company takes all the risk! It's that simple.

How can this be possible? Here's the answer: Insurance companies able to offer fixed indexed annuities are typically some of the strongest companies in the nation; they have not only an immense depth of financial resources, they also have the staying power to recover from any number of market drops because the company will be there for decades, even centuries to come. In other words, they have both the time and money to recover from a crash—after a certain age, we can't. The company therefore agrees to share a portion of gain, say, up to 6 percent to 8 percent of an up-market environment. You have nothing to lose. When the S&P tanks, you sit it out with a modest baseline rate of earnings (maybe 1%) until the market recovers and begins to rise again.

Looking at it another way, indexed annuities are fixed annuities that offer additional earning potential when times are good on the DOW. They still guarantee the safety of your principal, of course, but I really like the way they also protect the *money we make when the market is up*. Meaning, you can't lose what you've already made when the market goes down. And fixed indexed annuities almost always see significantly greater earnings than standard fixed annuities, making fixed *indexed* annuities one of the best safe-money alternatives around.

Returns from Fixed Indexed Annuities

I sometimes get repeat questions about this aspect of FIAs, so let me be clear: while fixed indexed annuities offer a share of market gains made by the insurance company, these gains may vary, given the ups and down on Wall Street we see every day. With variable annuities, you not only lose money in a declining market, your losses may continue until they eat away at your principal—people have lost a good deal of money in variable annuities.

Although variable annuities may offer higher returns in upside markets, variables are very much exposed to risk.

With fixed indexed annuities, you get the gain without the loss. Your fixed indexed annuity will essentially flat-line as the variable keeps on losing, potentially eroding principal in the variable annuity. Again, the fixed indexed annuity provides a modest level of added interest, *even when fixed indexed annuity earnings go flat*.

How much can fixed indexed annuities earn during market up-cycles? These products vary from carrier to carrier but they generally have excellent potential for strong earnings. In recent years, some fixed indexed annuities have returned up to 15 percent.

If the Dow returns 20 percent in a strong year and the insurance company earns 20 percent, will you get 20 percent as the owner of a fixed indexed annuity contract? The answer is no, of course, because you have wisely decided to let the insurance company take all the risk. You will see a healthy portion of the gain in this illustration, though not all. But let's envision the prospect of a market decline the following year, where the Dow drops 25 percent, thus annihilating all of last year's gains while dipping deeper into investor pockets. In this scenario, the 100-percent risk-exposed DOW investor has not only lost the 20 percent gain from last year, he lost another five percent as well, and even more in fees and administrative costs.

With a fixed indexed annuity, you would keep your contracted amount of gain when the market was up 20 percent. As it drops down 25 percent, you sit tight until conditions improve. *You get to keep your gains* from the period when times were good, without the mounds of fees and administrative charges associated with market risk.

Anyone taking a serious look at actual year-by-year data, tracking ups and downs among all market indexes over almost any significant time period will see one thing: People riding the Wall Street roller coaster saw roughly the same amount of gain as those holding fixed indexed annuity contracts. And the fixed indexed annuity did it without imposing all the brain damage of having to watch the Dow plummet, as the Dow loves to do from time to time.

"Just saying." Your call.

Other Invaluable Benefits of Fixed Indexed Annuities

Even before the conception of fixed indexed annuities, standard fixed annuities have been popular among pensioners from ancient Rome through more recent centuries in the British Empire due to the assurance of steady income in retirement.

Modern annuities—other than variables—provide **guaranteed safety of principal**, which is probably one of the more enduring qualities of the annuity.

Annuities also offer a **minimum guarantee of interest no matter what happens** to the market. Some standard annuities might offer slightly higher "fixed" interest earnings on an annual basis, as opposed to fixed indexed annuities, because standard fixed annuities do not entitle their owners to a share of earnings when the DOW soars. Yet, some fixed indexed annuities come close to those baseline guarantees, even while offering a substantial share of a given index.

Another important aspect of holding an annuity is **tax-deferral**. Rules differ from product to product but, basically, the annuity may be allowed to grow in value without being taxed until distributions begin.

An often-debated component of the annuity is **liquidity**. In the past, insurance companies levied heavy penalties for early withdrawal from some annuities. (To be fair, mutual funds and other risked-based accounts also charge hefty withdrawal penalties, while loading up on consumer fees and administrative charges.) In truth, many if not most annuities offer liberal thresholds of annual withdrawals during the life of the annuity. In fact, most products automatically let the annuity holder take out 10 percent per year, no questions asked, while a new generation of annuities offer increasingly consumer-friendly withdrawal penalties if you choose to withdraw *more than* 10 percent per year.

Some companies even offer **penalty-free withdrawals**, for example, and the annuity industry as a whole has been introducing more **liquidity options**.

Again, this is where the advice of an experienced annuity expert can be invaluable. People new to my business find what seems (to them) like a mind-boggling array of variation in product features, withdrawal policies and the rest. Not me. I was there when they were introduced. I've been there through the changes. I can talk about a wide array of products and features from experience and sheer memory when other planners are scrambling for guidebooks from the carrier.

Wherever you are, it's important to work with an annuity expert, not just a newbie who jumped on the bandwagon after the '08 crash. You'll know when you ask questions and they have to dive into a manual one too many times.

We've already covered the annuity's **lifetime-income guarantee**, which has become an extremely popular feature in recent years, for obvious reasons. Nobody wants to be forced out of retirement and back to work if they can help it. Lifetime income can protect you from that very situation. But not all annuities offer lifetime income options, and income options vary. Some income features provide an increased level of income for a period of time; others provide income for a surviving spouse after the annuitant passes away. I can guide you through the complex marketplace of annuities today and make sure we find the annuity tailor-made for you.

This is where the rubber meets the road in the New Normal of retirement planning.

As I said earlier, it takes more than just one conversation for anyone to professionally delve into the annuity marketplace on a client's behalf. I often require several meetings, going into considerable detail about client lifestyles and finances. Only then would I begin shopping for appropriate annuity products for you, along with the myriad of features that tend to go with them.

I have spent years perfecting the proprietary discovery process I now use to ensure the best fit for my clients. As you might imagine, it took years for me to learn how to assemble everything an advisor needs to know before looking at products and features.

What I'm trying to say is this: If you find yourself in the company of someone who somehow happens to "know you from the start," be wary. If they say they "know just the annuity for you" without taking the time to conduct several meetings, get a second opinion. I can't say that enough. A true financial professional will spend most of his or her time getting to know you and, because they know the market so well, much less time digging through product lines to find the right fit for your situation.

We've probably said enough for the purposes of this book about the annuity's **participation in growth during up-markets on Wall Street**. Just know that share percentages vary, some offering higher baseline growth no matter what happens, in exchange for a slightly lower share of upside gains. Others offer good gains and more liberal, or even penalty-free, early withdrawal policies, and the list continues. Let me know and I will send along more information, or you can come in for a one-on-one meeting.

As for your beneficiaries and legacy planning, annuities **avoid probate** which has made them a favored anti-probate tool among estate planners. While almost all annuities do this, imagine the alternative: leaving cash in the bank or bonds in a safe deposit box after you pass away. (Don't even think about it. Avoid probate with annuities.)

In days gone by, annuities were basically one-trick ponies with limited options. Today, modern annuities offer a smorgasbord of **custom features** to enhance flexibility, reduce withdrawal fees, increase earnings, and more. These include: **guaranteed growth rates, life time income**—based on income for either one or both spouses—**death benefits** and **enhanced protection against health care costs**.

Annual Resets

I'm often asked how earnings are protected in fixed indexed annuities, and how those earnings are calculated. The answer is a concept called the "annual reset."

The greater percentage of indexed annuities use the annual reset strategy, which allows earned interest to be "locked in" every year. At the end of that year, the value of the index will be reset, which means that any future stock market decrease will not affect the value of interest already earned. In situations where market volatility triggers fluctuating returns on Wall Street, interest already earned by the annuity would not be affected.

It also increases the value of the policyholder's asset and allows the index account to be increased by an index credit. This happens on the annual anniversary date stipulated in the contract. Again, this credit is locked in and cannot be lost due to adverse market conditions. As such, it creates a new bottom-line for future earnings. The index credit adds to your original principal, which is used to re-enter the market—now with a higher level of earning potential—when moving forward as the market grows in value. As the value of the index grows in an upside market, the value of your account will increase from the point of last reset. It basically acts like compounding interest, but is based on upside activity in the market.

Looking at it from another angle, this extremely advantageous strategy will allow you to avoid market losses if the market declines during the year. The account simply continues from that point forward—before the decline—which puts the account holder in an ideal position since he/she can participate in the market without risk of loss. The annuity account with an annual reset feature provides that the account will not have to recover previous losses in order for the annuity to qualify for added earnings.

For each contract year, the ending value of the index becomes the new starting point of value for the following year—an ideal situation in my opinion.

Income Riders

Sometimes called "lifetime income riders" or "lifetime income benefit riders," these features allow policyholders to receive a steady income for life without having to risk the loss of their retirement assets. The income rider is a stipulation attached to an annuity that provides investment safety, income guarantees and ultimately peace of mind for people worried about running out of money in retirement.

It may be desirable to look for the income rider when purchasing an annuity, if lifetime income is the kind of feature you wish to include in your retirement plan. Insurance companies will offer such an option before you buy the policy, and the rider makes income possible because, in place of receiving annuitized payments from your annuity, your income results from regular withdrawals. At the same time, most riders will set a guaranteed amount of growth for your annuity, which is based on a guaranteed income percentage multiplied by the value of your account. The income percentage is set according to your age at the time you decide to begin receiving payments from the annuity.

*   *   *

Regardless of the features you choose for your fixed indexed annuity, your lifetime income will have the protection of guaranteed growth. Your principal investment will have a shield against market risk, and periodic market gains will be locked-in against loss. Your account value will move up when the market moves ahead and this type of annuity can accordingly create income you cannot outlive.

Regardless of how much money you made during your working years, or how you built your retirement portfolio before retirement, the most important thing you can do *in retirement* is to change the methods you once used to manage your money during your working years. Retirement money is "know-so" money and in the New Normal of retirement finance, fixed indexed annuities have become a proven method of managing your retirement, without having to fear the disastrous consequences of market losses.

It's all about coming to terms with the New Normal of retirement planning. Forget about the old days of traditional pension plans and living off income based on stocks and bonds. The rules have changed. We're in a different economy. New technologies have reduced the odds of winning for average investors; even seasoned professionals are increasingly challenged by sudden shifts in political winds overseas and other factors, things we never had to worry about in the past.

As workers face downsizing from companies streamlining the workplace, our earning years are challenged by the fact that people are living longer than ever before. Yet, retirement planning tools available today are more advanced, ready to meet the challenge of the years ahead. All you need to do is trim your lifestyle according to an income managed by risk-free assets like annuities. To do that more effectively, you need someone like me. I've already done the legwork, the research and the thousands of hours of meetings, learning from decades of clients precisely how to safeguard your retirement with the maximum lifestyle possible.

After all, it's really about the way you approach your life from this point forward. When it comes to the bottom line, it's all about enjoyment, even more than money, and the joy of knowing you will have peace of mind for the rest of your life.

CHAPTER EIGHT

"Color" Your Carefree Retirement

I believe that everyone in this nation has a common goal. Regardless of our financial circumstances we all want to retire successfully. But in order to achieve that goal we first need to establish what our desired income is going to be when we reach retirement age, and that's the challenge. In retirement, we must adopt a new Money-Mindset, so in this chapter we're going to look at a more detailed approach to "color-coded" retirement planning.

The challenge is to pre-determine the source of our retirement income. *Exactly* where will it come from as we head into our retirement years? This important question applies to everyone approaching retirement or already in retirement, and one of your income sources will probably be Social Security.

We'll take a good look at Social Security—past, present and future—and how we must prepare to deal with the changing nature of SSI (Social Security Income) in the future. We also want to look at the "one constant," which involves a simple equation. Most of us relate retirement to the accumulation of a large nest egg, which would sustain us in our retirement years: That is, the bigger the nest-egg the better our quality of life throughout retirement.

Have you heard this before? We all have, but this kind of thinking tends to overlook one critical issue: What type of nest egg are we accumulating?

In other words, what "color" is the money in your retirement portfolio? We touched on this issue before. Now, let's take a closer look.

It all depends upon variable circumstances but theoretically, it would appear that the larger your retirement account the larger your income will be in retirement. Unfortunately, this may not come true. The manner in which your dollars are allocated—i.e. the "color" of your money—will make *a real* difference in your ultimate financial outcome. The "color of money" is, in fact, a recurring theme in this book because it reflects one of the most important concepts in the New Normal.

Risk is the obvious element that would make or break your upcoming retirement experience. We've all witnessed, first hand, the consequences of risk in extreme circumstances including the Wall Street Crash of 2008 and the ensuing years of ongoing recession.

More recently, the market has been rising. The economy is apparently beginning to solidify. Never mind November and December of 2012 when it appeared that Congress and the White House were going to bicker until the nation fell off the Fiscal Cliff, which could trigger another recession according media pundits. Hard to imagine our own politicians allowing something like that to happen—it didn't—but allowing us to teeter on the edge due to sheer, partisan posturing shows just how precarious the New Financial Normal can really be. Only a few years ago and against all economic wisdom, the banking world decided to create bad loans in a sub-prime mortgage bubble and re-package them as popular but relatively worthless securities, which helped to fuel an economic crisis of a magnitude unseen since the Great Depression. The lesson: Human nature is both predictable and unpredictable, and along the way we hear all sorts of advice about how to allocate our hard-earned life savings for retirement.

When people first step into my office, some of them lack a clear understanding of how their money is actually allocated. Some have been put into investment programs without receiving enough explanation of what sort of investments the programs contain. In fact, investments in various programs may change radically without a client's knowledge, resulting in a radical increase of risk as trades are implemented at lightning speed through electronic trading networks and the like.

A few years ago, an erratic glitch in the nation's electronic trading system led to a 1,000-point drop in the DOW/S&P over a matter of hours, during which billions of dollars were lost.

During the Crash of 2008, highly reactive markets plunged. Substantial losses meant some retirement accounts were reduced by 70 percent, 80 percent and more. This happened, in my opinion, because the overwhelming hope for potential flash-profits in the market caused millions of investors to abandon common sense. Saving for a rainy day was a thing of the past. Many people were averse to common-sense strategies safeguarding life savings that assure modest gains on a virtual loss-proof platform, which we will discuss at length later on.

Instead, they let their brokers do the work for them, in the open market, without taking a good, hard look at how much risk they were taking. Then it was too late. This, too, was the result of failure to see the true color of money.

While the same, persistent kind of optimism has—at this writing—been luring some people back to market risk and volatility, a great many others have learned from experience. They have been moving in droves to sound, steady retirement plans, which ironically allow a degree of market participation and respectable earnings—without the risk!

The latter are the types of investment programs we like to offer. They will help you realize a nice retirement lifestyle upon which you can depend—no matter what happens down the road.

The Color of Your Money: Defined

So, what is the color of your money? Almost every one of us will say, "Green," but I'm about to change that perception.

When placing money in an arena where value can either soar or plunge overnight, this kind of money is colored Red because it symbolizes risk. All sorts of investments put us in the "red" zone from real estate investment trusts to various stocks and bonds. We all know the signs marking the "red" zone. When approaching the zone, I simply ask people to "Stop and Look Carefully" at the numbers. Consider the backbone of the company or organization you are about to plunge into with your hard-earned savings.

Next, we encounter more moderate risk environments where risk is a bit less precipitous, although present and still prone to radical swings in markets both domestic and overseas. This is considered a "Yellow," or moderate-risk environment. In this area, I caution people to "Pay Attention" because this type of risk vehicle requires constant vigilance. If you enter this part of the market, going into conservative bonds, etc., do so with the understanding that YOU must maintain a constant eye on your own money. Don't plan to sit back and rely on someone you may not be able to reach by phone for several days, if ever.

As mentioned previously, the final color to be explored is "Green." Most of us think of all money as being green but now we have a different perspective. Truly "Green" money is going to work for us in a place where you and your retirement vehicle may proceed safely. This is a place where risky traffic is minimal. You will move ahead at a sane, steady pace, without risking a collision with unforeseen economic events.

When we think of a traffic light, we think of heeding red, yellow and green lights because we know what will happen if we don't. The same goes for investing and saving for retirement.

- **Red means: "Stop and Look Carefully"**
- **Yellow means: "Pay Attention"**
- **Green means: "Safe to Proceed"**

"Financially Color-Blind" Means Trouble for Retirees

Many traditional brokers avoid thinking about the color of your money. They're intent on talking about the next investment product we should buy, which typically involve investment management teams with supposed market wizardry and the ability to predict the future of risk. They will talk about gain versus loss, investment sectors and global economic trends. They will show you charts and graphs pointing to optimistic levels of *anticipated* profit—in unseen worlds ahead where elaborate theories supposedly mitigate risk.

For people in or near retirement, I don't buy it, neither should you.

When you focus on a particular product rather than the color of that investment, it could very easily change your retirement landscape in an undesirable way.

On the other hand, you may run into brokers who do talk about the color of risk when introducing certain investment products. If they do, fine, but do they really get into the minutia, the fine print and intricate detail describing precisely what kind of financial risk you are about to take? Probably not. More likely than not, they'll get all excited about things like "ground-floor opportunities" and "hot" new products and emerging market opportunities. This is what they are trained to do. This is how they think. When they talk about "color," they're often talking about Red and Yellow—Stop and Look Carefully versus Pay Attention—because most products they introduce involve the possibility of losing your money (not theirs, by the way). Some of these people never fully grasp the true meaning of a "green" investment, which is not in your best interest, especially when you are in or near retirement.

As we move into our pre-retirement years, we must focus on color because it can greatly affect your retirement landscape.

The Speed Bumps of Life

If life was all about smooth sailing with perfect guarantees at the end of the road, nobody would worry about planning anything. But we all know about the little speed bumps along the way, and how unexpected events can seriously affect our best planning.

This pertains to financial planning, in particular. In the last decade, people thought they had it all down pat, that their investments in securities, mutual funds, bonds and real estate were a sure thing—a hedge against inflation with a solid retirement at the end of their working years.

Then a very large company called Enron collapsed, and with it went the retirement dreams of people who banked their savings on Enron shares. Unfortunately, many others had invested in Enron and they lost large parts of their retirement portfolios as the company went down. Around the same time, the unthinkable happened and telecommunications giant WorldCom took a dive in 2002, followed by the indictment of Martha Stewart for insider trading in 2003, which put a new light on the inner world of investment and the way things often work against the average Joe and his investment portfolio. Around that time, the market took a real nose dive and dropped 21 percent, which could have been re-captured over a period of a few years, or many years, which is fine if you have a long working life ahead of you.

But again, what if you don't? Today, for many pre-retirees and people already in retirement, if you lost 21 percent in the market, it wouldn't necessarily be re-captured by another 21 percent gain. Not when you're dealing with a loss of principal, as you are when you're in your retirement years; the equation is more like 27 percent. After losing principal, it takes a 27 percent recovery to cover a 21 percent loss.

In this situation, it becomes quite difficult to re-capture that kind of loss without taking on more and more risk. So, it's the old vicious cycle: The more you lose, the more you feel you have to risk, the more you stand to lose due to greater risk. People who slip into this kind of loss-and-recovery cycle sometime wind up losing it all. And we're talking about more or less normal market risks, which absolutely can and do hit a wall from time to time, leading to big losses for investors—which is fine if you have many years remaining in the workplace to recover.

Or is it *fine* for working people? How many significant loss periods can we sustain over a period of, say, 30 years and still expect an adequate retirement lifestyle?

Even people in their working years should consider a few options to pure risk. Maybe they could set aside money in vehicles that would guarantee principal and a certain level of gain, while enduring other kinds of risk in things like company 401(k)s—before the time comes to roll it all into Green vehicles with income guarantees.

As for retirees and pre-retirees, the risk-loss-recovery syndrome is unacceptable.

Even in apparently steady markets, someone like Bernie Madoff comes along with a devastating scheme which, in 2008, stripped his clients of everything they had. This happened due to a basic Ponzi scheme, enacted by someone who had been highly respected in the financial world . . . until he wasn't. Around the same time—with or without Madoff's influence—the investors panicked again and the result was a 35-percent market drop, which meant that many investors would need to regain 53 percent in the market to recover.

People come into my office still reeling from the Madoff swindle and the crash of 2008. To this day, they have not recovered those losses. They are still struggling to get back where they were.

Fail to Prepare and Face the Consequences

No one knows what will happen in the near future, from the years 2013 and beyond.

We face many unknowns as our national economy becomes increasingly integrated with global economies beyond our shores. At the same time, we continue to climb out of a lingering recession as we grapple with increasing national debt and what could become a constant specter of tax increases and inflation.

This and other factors mean we could be looking at ongoing, turbulent times for many years to come. On the bright side, however, financial professionals and investment opportunities are more attuned to ways we can manage our savings through troubled times. At this writing, certain sectors of the economy are showing new signs of life: Housing prices seem to be improving; the stock market has managed to hold on to a significant rebound and employment figures are beginning to improve.

No one really knows what to expect over the long-term horizon, but we have always had some level of uncertainty, even during the best of times. I can say, however, and with a degree of certainty, that our regional, national and global economies are in for more volatility than they were before the crash. We see that volatility in the Euro. I keep reading about Spain being on the verge of financial collapse. Greece is teetering at the edge with massive unemployment and no real plan to pull itself out of a growing depression. Italy is beginning to have problems, too, and all three nations seem to be linked to a subtle domino effect. As one of the three begins to fall, some economists think others may follow. How long will nations like Germany be able to join hands with major banking organizations to gamble on debt in Italy, Greece and Spain? Will other nations join the list of endangered economies? Given all of the above, can the U.S. indefinitely sustain a strong economy with China as a major lender?

The short answer: If your retirement is protected by "Green" money: *who cares?*

We're definitely tied to a troubled, global-financial community. We will continue to struggle with this phenomenon. It's part of the New Normal. Guess what? Times change, all you have to do is take it into account and plan for it.

So much for global financial turmoil in the Red-Money Zone: What are *you* doing for yourself, and your family, in preparation for the way things will likely be for years to come? I hope you'll agree that I've touched on real solutions you can implement today. All you have to do is act before another "speed bump" comes along.

Historically from early 2000 to early 2011, one basic phenomenon is clear: As the S&P dropped from 2000 through 2003 the corresponding amount of cash needed to rebound was significant. Investors lost a bucket of money during the 2000 to 2003 "correction period," and they lost it in less than a year.

Note that the drop beginning around 2000 continued for a three-year period, when markets finally began to rise again, from 2003 until 2008. We know what happened then: The period beginning in autumn 2008 gave the term "fall" an all-new meaning. The "fall" of 2008 sent the market tumbling downward at a speed unprecedented since the Great Depression.

While the market dropped nearly 40 percent from late 2008 through mid-2009, the now overshadowed 2000-2003 decline was sharp, devastating and left investors facing a financial mountain to climb in order to recover. In 2003, alone, the market had taken a 21 percent nose-dive from the prior year, which signaled a moment of market turmoil and uncertainty.

All I can say is that it happened again on a more precipitous downward incline beginning in 2008, when a 40 percent drop meant investors needed a near 60-percent recovery to break even.

The chart further illustrates that by 2012, the market had still failed to fully recover from losses endured from 2008 to 2009. Far from it. The market in 2012 was still some 12 points down from late 2008. People were wondering if they would ever recover after such a swift, unsettling ride.

Further aggravating the problem was a perceived and related need to take on more risk, after having lost so much from the same kind of risk-based financial strategy. Some people were convinced that they should actually double up on risk to regain losses from the '08 crash, further exposing themselves to more of the same in the future.

It might have temporarily worked for some people, but they would have been strapped to the same doubled-up risk until the next drop comes around. That's the problem. People forget the past, forgetting to protect themselves from known market cycles.

People using New Normal strategies have learned from experience.

Let's imagine two individuals: One is younger and in his earning years with a significant time horizon ahead. The other is older, in retirement, and taking income from a portfolio based on the same types of investments. Both are riding the S&P, but the elder receiving income sees his income drop accordingly after a sharp drop in the market.

Because we tend to lock-in to a certain retirement lifestyle, when the market drops the elder receiving income ignores the need to decrease his spending—in order to adjust his retirement lifestyle to market conditions. This is understandable. It can be very difficult to chip away at things we're used to having, things we enjoy, let alone household costs and other personal expenses. Making life even more difficult, in this scenario things like property taxes are set in stone; they begin to take an increasingly significant chunk out of our elder's total income. Yet, he still clings to the same lifestyle, expecting better returns on his investments.

What can happen in this situation? Almost invariably (and statistically), during a market drop we tend to dip into principal to make up for the loss of income. In other words, if we fail to decrease the income to which we've become accustomed, our principal will continue to erode. This happens when you base your original retirement income on the higher value of your retirement savings. You set yourself up for significant problems with your retirement account. As you continue to take income during any kind of market downturn, the depletion of your principal picks up increasing speed.

What this means in the end is that you will eventually have to reduce your income, one way or another. Your lifestyle will suffer. Some people will run out of money altogether.

If you find yourself in this situation, visualize a red light in a traffic intersection. Red means: "Stop and Look Carefully." It's time to convert risk to lifetime income, before it's too late.

In the upcoming pages, you will understand how to take your retirement from red-light status to green-light peace of mind. But first, let's further define "red, yellow and green" in terms of working investment vehicles.

In the "red" category we have things like stocks, mutual funds and Electronically Traded Funds or ETFs.

In the "yellow" category are certain fixed-indexed annuities and indexed life insurance policies, which require attention. We need to monitor their performance.

In the "green" category come bank Certificates of Deposit, fixed annuities and annuities *with lifetime income features* or income riders.

Back to the red zone, again we call red money our "hope so" money. Our retiree above is lost in Hope-So-Land. His money is immersed in market exposure that he hopes will do well indefinitely (because he isn't ready to trim his lifestyle in a downturn). We hope our red money would be there for us in retirement when we really need it, but it can quickly evaporate.

Our green money is "know-so" money, because we know how it will perform; we know it will be there for us in retirement no matter what. We know the rate it will pay and when payouts will be received. In other words, green money in the form of things like income-producing annuities will be there while accruing interest.

In the middle, we have our "yellow" money. Yellow money is a sort of hybrid between red and green monies because it can have some of the best of both worlds. Yellow money would go into fixed-indexed annuities and indexed life insurance because they protect principal while providing a link between income products and the market itself. In fact, these vehicles can allow for a considerable amount of market gain, which would go into your principal, while putting on the brakes if the market begins to slide, thus protecting your principal until the market begins to rise again.

As you can see, our yellow-money category is quite attractive for many coming into retirement as well as those already in retirement. People in both groups may choose to keep some of their assets in green, "know-so" money, or even a bit in the "red." But far more will lean toward the yellow, since green money earns little, while red puts money at risk, pure and simple. How much risk should we be taking in retirement? We'll address that issue in a moment.

Risk and Asset Allocation

First, let's examine the way some financial people would put your money into a mix of investments. Some planners might want to put your money into a mix of red money. Others might mix all of the colors—red, yellow and green—but you might not know how much red, for example, has gone into the mix. This is one way to approach risk and asset allocation, but it's not the only way.

Here's another way to approach allocation of retirement funds, with a more rock-solid kind of planning. We call it: G.A.P. This stands for Guarantees, Allocation and Protection. Do you have G.A.P in the foundation of your retirement plan? Putting it another way . . .

- **Do you have solid guarantees to safeguard your retirement money, no matter what?**
- **Do you have the right kind of allocation to protect your money from risk?**
- **Do you have solid protection against losing your money in down markets?**

The presence of all of the above is what we call G.A.P.

In order to create a proper G.A.P. in your retirement plan, we must take an honest look at the alternative.

When money is in the "red" category, it's invested in risk, of course, including stocks, bonds, real estate trusts, mutual funds and more. Historic market downturns show what can happen to red money. Many of us have known, or have personally experienced, having red money at the wrong time, which can be almost any time. As we discussed earlier, future economies and global financial interaction will definitely impact red money in the future. We know that. It's a given. Markets have been extremely volatile when least expected, regardless of the usual consortium of upbeat analysis in the financial media. We have also seen periods when loss led to markets that recovered. But recoveries have been followed by big drops, where losses were offset by inadequate periods of recovery.

After the great crash of 2008, retirees have emerged with a more balanced mind-set. After losses sustained by so many people, we naturally want to have some sort of recovery mechanism built into our portfolios—a mechanism based on certain guarantees.

The momentum behind the desire for safety and market participation therefore led to a New Normal wave of hybrid strategies—retirement plans based on "yellow" vehicles.

Since the crash, we've seen the market surge, followed by declines, some more significant than others. Many of my clients have enjoyed both periods because they've been riding the middle, or yellow, category. Through market declines, they never lost a penny; their accounts simply flat-lined until the market recovered. As the market finally began to come back, their accounts began to come back with respectable returns, shedding light on a most important phenomenon: Through the "up" periods, their accounts accumulated value; through the "down" periods, their accounts lost *zero* value. Through both up and down periods combined, and beyond, their accounts have seen, and will continue to see, steadily accumulating value—without fear of risk and, more importantly, without the loss!

In short, they were able to keep all of the earnings gained during the "up" periods, without sacrificing the same earnings during "down" periods. You're probably beginning to glimpse the potential for something else . . . stability of income.

While many variations run with the theme outlined above, let's look at one specific type of product and the numbers attached. I know of a fixed-index annuity that produced an annual income of $10,524 *for life*. This occurred after a client made an initial principal contribution of $100,000, which grew to an accumulation value of 136,000 over a ten-year period. Yet the "income rider value" grew to $210,000, again allowing for a $10,524 income guaranteed for life. At the same time, this account allowed a six-percent annual withdrawal per year from principal.

While the account holder enjoyed his guaranteed income, remember the previously discussed S&P market volatility during the same time period—from 2000 through 2010?

During that period, risk-based accounts in the market dropped from $100,000 down to $60,000 from 2000 through 2003. As our *guaranteed-income client* enjoyed steady increases in accumulation value and income rider-value throughout, the risk-based account might have recovered from 2003 to 2008 but catastrophe happened all over again, in a single year, wiping out all recovery attained by the risk-based account during the previous five-year period!

Because market recovery fails to fully recapture loss, the risk-based account initially worth $100,000 was worth only $85,640 after 10 agonizing years of market swings, and it had little to show for the anguish.

Meanwhile, the fixed index annuity—the *guaranteed-income account*—not only accumulated value, it left the owner with a *guaranteed income for life* of $10,524.

The scenario outlined above clearly shows why so many people in or near retirement have opted for the fixed index annuity. All sorts of options and products fall under the fixed-index category and while the color of your money may be yellow with this kind of product, various options offer a variety of features to further empower your retirement lifestyle. Next, we'll uncover a secret weapon for your guaranteed-income plan.

CHAPTER NINE

The Power of "Product X"

For now let's call it "Product X." I'll show you how it works.

When you put assets into Product X, they will not be available for use until you reach the age of 62. From this point forward, for every year that you wait to begin taking income from Product X, the value of Product X will increase by 6.25 percent annually until you reach your retirement age. That's impressive growth, indeed! If, after you reach retirement age, you continue to delay the taking of assets from Product X, up to the age of 70, your income will increase by 8 percent per year. That's almost unheard of for many a fixed-income product.

Once you begin to take income from Product X, your income will be guaranteed for life. However, Product X has a significant limitation: When you die, no more income would be available from Product X. Without proper planning, all income would disappear, leaving nothing for your family.

We all know the identity of Product X: It's Social Security, of course. As we all know, Social Security comes with a wide array of specific rules and guidelines, all of which can affect the income you would get from Social Security.

Before you begin to draw from Social Security, it is most important to do your homework because a good deal of customization can go into your Social Security plan, which can allow for an extremely important role in the amount of income you ultimately receive.

The Social Security Debate

The future shape and existence of the Social Security program itself has been one of the most hotly debated issues before Congress in recent years.

Some members of Congress look at assets garnered by the program as a cash cow to be siphoned off for other federal programs. Other congressional leaders look at Social Security as a cumbersome entitlement program. They think those of us who paid into the program for a lifetime are somehow not entitled to payback from our accounts.

Congressional plans for Social Security remain in question.

In my opinion, people in or near retirement today would be able to rely on Social Security income, although annual Cost Of Living Adjustments (COLAs) may not exist in the future within the Social Security program. This is one area where the nature of Social Security will always remain in question. After two years without COLAs, from 2010 to 2012, Social Security payments were finally increased by 3.6 percent. Of course, 2012 was an election year, which may or may not have affected the granting of a COLA adjustment.

That's only one of several issues we must consider when looking at Social Security as our sole means of income in retirement.

Social Security Timeline

Many of us look at Social Security as a time-honored, historic program that will always be there when we need it. In truth, when looking over the broad landscape of human history, Social Security is a relatively new program, which has changed considerably in scope and detail since its inception in 1940.

In 1940, Ida Mae Fuller received the first federally sanctioned monthly benefit check from the Social Security program. Her monthly check amounted to $22.40, and by 1950, after the culmination of World War II a need was realized to increase Social Security payments in order to keep payments current with inflation.

In 1950, President Harry Truman signed the first Social Security amendment, which allowed for the first COLA. Social Security payments were now on track to keep pace with inflation. Then a need was realized for some workers to begin receiving early retirement checks from Social Security.

In 1961, President John F. Kennedy signed Social Security amendments allowing all workers to begin early retirement at age 62, but with reduced benefits.

Amendments continued in 1972, when President Richard Nixon signed a law authorizing increased COLA adjustments. Effective in September of that year, procedures were established to issue automatic Cost Of Living

Adjustments, which would begin in 1975, which was a significant move back then because inflation was growing quickly. Inflation was at the forefront of public opinion and was a widely voiced discussion related to Social Security payments.

Those were good years for Social Security, but things would begin to change for a program once guaranteed by Franklin D. Roosevelt to remain in place tax-free for all Americans.

In 1983, President Ronald Reagan signed into law amendments that would allow for the gradual increase of the retirement age under Social Security from 65 to 67. The increase would occur over several years, but Reagan's move is significant because it suggests that government officials suspected vulnerability in the program. For the first time, they began to realize that at the current rate of income payouts, the Social Security program may not last.

Reagan was perhaps the first president to face facts about the program and do something to solidify its future.

By 1991, the government began to mail annual Social Security statements to all workers over 25; statements calculated an individual's future Social Security income at a current rate of contribution into the program.

In 2000, President Bill Clinton signed a law eliminating a task called the Retirement Earnings Test for Social Security beneficiaries above full retirement age. In 2011, the Social Security Administration stopped the issuance of annual Social Security statements to Social Security recipients, thus saving the government $75 million per year.

This happened at a time when Social Security beneficiaries were accustomed to receiving their statements, but cost cuts were necessary in a program that would see many more in the coming years. Not that we can't receive our statements because they are easily located and viewed online, and we can still ask for them by mail—they are simply not sent automatically.

Further erosion of funds supporting the Social Security Administration can be seen through the years. In 1950, for example, the Social Security Administration indicates that 16.5 working Americans served each Social Security recipient—that's how many people were paying into the system for every person in retirement receiving benefits.

The Increasing Burden on Social Security

Today, only 2.9 workers serve each recipient, which amounts to 157 million people in the workplace, who serve 55 million people in retirement receiving benefits. This means that 157 million people are in the workplace funding Social Security through annual taxation, while 55 million are receiving Social Security benefits. Much of the radical shift in the worker-to-recipient ratio has occurred due to the explosive birth of the Baby Boom generation of the late 1940s and beyond. But the problem is further aggravated by the millions removed from the work force by the recent—some say ongoing—recession-ridden years since 2008. Bottom line, far more people are drawing from the Social Security program. Far fewer people have been paying into it since the aftermath of World War II.

Many of us feel truly entitled to Social Security benefits and rightly so. After all, millions of Americans now entering their retirement years have been paying into the Social Security system for their entire working lives. Seniors now in retirement have paid into the system as well.

As we receive paychecks during our working years most of us automatically pay into the Social Security system. The system was established in 1935 by Franklin D. Roosevelt as a way to ensure that seniors would receive something to live on in their golden years. After the heartbreaking years of the Great Depression, Americans gladly went along with the idea of a Social Security system. It was, and still is, a good system, one of the government programs in place that works for Americans in spite of the numerous ways Social Security coffers have been tapped through the years to bolster other government programs. But again, that's reality.

To this day, 6.2 percent of our working salary is paid by the employee for Social Security while the employer pays in 6.2 percent. The breakdown works like this: For every $1,130 you make in a given year, you get one credit toward receiving Social Security benefits. Although you may earn only four (4) credits per year, a minimum of 40 credits will be needed in order for you to become eligible for benefits.

After a lifetime of paying into the Social Security system, the average monthly benefit was approximately $1,229 per month, while the maximum allowable benefit was $2,513. The way your Social Security benefits are calculated is based on your highest 35 years of earnings in the workplace. For those who have worked less than 35 years, their missing years at work are counted as zero. No matter how much money you might have made per year, the maximum taxable income for Social Security benefits has been $110,100, which helps to explain why maximum benefits paid out currently come to roughly $2,500 per month.

But the overall health of the Social Security system is something we all face.

At this writing, a great deal of political wrangling over the future of Social Security leaves many wondering when benefits might be reduced, or even cut off. For the foreseeable future, it appears that those age 55 and over will continue to receive benefits under the current system, but give us a call for updates because you never know. Everything in the system seems to be up for grabs in a post-recession environment where politicians scramble to find ways to pay off a mountain of federal debt. For example, people in the 60-plus-age bracket saw the Social Security Administration halt the mailing of statements in 2011, although now it appears that people over 60 might begin receiving their statements in the mail again. The rest of the population will be challenged, however, to determine the amount of benefits they would receive, so it's important to note that related information can be found at www.ssa.gov, although it may take several steps to find your own personal information. You can also call the Social Security Administration, or you can work with a financial service professional, which can be an important plus when planning your retirement using Social Security benefits.

The information above is cited to point out the questionable future of Social Security: While they took out mailed statements, the resulting savings were a drop in a rain barrel compared to the drain on Social Security today.

Americans Rely on Social Security

Today, at least 90 percent of Americans age 65 and older are receiving Social Security benefits. While Social Security makes up roughly 41 percent of total income for Americans in retirement, many seniors rely solely on Social Security benefits. Meaning, this is all they have, and this reality comes at a time when a huge influx of Baby Boomers are crowding into the system as they look for ways to sustain their retirement lifestyles. Further aggravating the situation is the reality of retirement portfolios lost during the crash of 2008. While many Baby Boomers were never particularly good at saving for retirement, a good number of them certainly were. Either way, we now have an enormous number of people without enough money to retire at all—they may be in dire need of their Social Security benefits at a time when those benefits could be challenged by Congress.

Obviously, a great many people must look very carefully at ways they can maximize their Social Security benefits. In this case, timing can mean everything. If you time your entry into the Social Security system incorrectly, it will cost you. If you start taking Social Security benefits too early, you stand to lose 57 percent of the benefits you would have received had you waited until a later time.

A Walk-Through-Tour of Social Security

This would happen if you begin taking your Social Security benefits at the age of 62, well ahead of the generally recommended retirement age of 66. People born in 1943 or after—up until 1954—*currently* receive full benefits at age 66. So, if you do decide to receive early benefits at age 62, your Primary Insurance Amount (PIA) benefit would be reduced. According to your lifespan, this amount could be greatly reduced, up to 57 percent.

Exactly how long would this reduced benefit be in place? It would remain fixed at a significant reduction of benefits *for a lifetime.* That's right: Make the wrong choice, jump in too early, and you cannot go back.

On the other hand, if you wait *beyond* the currently determined age required to receive full benefits, which is age 66, you would increase your benefits: Wait until age 67 (if you were born between 1943 and 1959) and you would get 108 percent of the benefit you would get at 66. Wait until age

70 and you would receive *132 percent* of benefits you would have taken at age 66, or $1,320 versus $1,000 a month—based on a PIA of $1,000.

This is important stuff that should be thoroughly examined with your financial professional when calculating your retirement needs. This is where things get dicey. If you have nothing other than Social Security to rely on for income, you may need the money early; you would definitely need it at age 66. In other words, you would have no choice.

If you jump in and begin strategizing with a financial professional, it could make all the difference. You might be able to come up with a plan for income allowing for a strategic delay in taking your Social Security benefits. This would be especially true for people with a history of longevity in the family, because a good many of us now *well live past our 70s* and into our 80s or 90s—and beyond. One's health can change at any time, of course, so we always face a certain amount of risk when delaying Social Security benefits, but consider the risk when you delay the planning process to ensure other sources of income and income-increasing strategies.

Either way, the process of change was apparently built into the Social Security system. President John F. Kennedy—always a Social Security advocate—clearly stated the importance of "well-being" that the Social Security program "plays . . . in providing for families, children and older persons living in times of stress." Yet, he went on to say that changes "in our population, in our working habits, and in our standard of living require constant revisions . . ." of the Social Security system. While many point out that FDR at one point indicated that Social Security benefits would not be taxed—not true today—he never said that the system would never face changes, especially during future economic climates over which he would have no control.

Among those items subject to change is the Cost of Living Adjustment (COLA) mentioned earlier. We saw a recent cessation of COLAs shortly after the crash of '08 and we'll likely see more. But for the foreseeable future, the history of COLAs under the Social Security program have generally hovered around 2 percent to 3 percent per year, although in some years they have dipped to 1.3 percent (in 1986) and soared to 14.3 percent (in 1980).

Given that perspective, it's interesting to note that in all the years from 1975 through 2011, only two years—2009 and 2010—received zero COLAs. This means that Social Security benefits have no real, enduring guarantee of being increased to keep up with inflation. Unlike a good many financial instruments out there today, Social Security benefits could remain static if future economies fall into another downturn—or if lawmakers determine a lack of COLAs to be in the best interest of federal deficit reduction.

Again, it's all up for grabs.

In summary, we can begin taking Social Security benefits anywhere between the age of 62 and 70. In the year 2012, the average American received $1,229 per month, with the Social Security benefit maximum set at $2,513. But it's particularly amazing to me that roughly 50 percent of Americans take the big hit: They begin taking early Social Security benefits at age 62. Despite the possibility of seeing a 57 percent reduction in benefits over a lifetime they do it anyway, probably because the initial hit is only a 25 percent benefit reduction during the first year, but this can change, according to how long we live.

Another statistic is also worth noting: At least 74 percent of retirees currently receive *reduced* benefits of some kind.

Back to the 50 percent who take their Social Security benefits at 62, why is this number so high? To me, it's an obvious indicator that a good many people in their 60s need income. This is probably due in part to the effects of a recession and not only unemployment but the fact that our dramatically reduced workplace may be particularly hard on people in their 50s and, especially, in their 60s.

While unemployment numbers finally began to shrink after the crash—at least through 2012—employers became increasingly accustomed to consolidation of their workforce, by increasing the workload on each worker, thus demanding a younger worker in some cases, who would work for less than their elder counterparts. Putting it another way, many in their 60s may be fully ready to go back to work but fewer jobs are available for elder workers. At the same time, some in this age category may be in poor health, after an era when job loss meant a loss of health coverage and related hardship across the board. Those in poor health also may feel that they won't live long enough to make the Full Retirement Age benefit worthwhile.

But my strongest suspicion is that most people are simply uninformed about Social Security benefits. They assume that 62 is the proper age to begin taking benefits, which also may be a choice driven by emotion.

For those reasons and more, at least 74 percent of people aged 62 and above have *voluntarily* chosen to receive reduced benefits by taking benefits earlier than age 66. If you look beyond the numbers, you will sense another dynamic in the works: People clearly rely on their Social Security benefits, perhaps more than ever before, since so many are cut out of the workplace before the traditional retirement at age 65. They cling to the hope that Social Security will always be there for us, despite an ongoing bout of saber-rattling to the contrary on Capitol Hill. So, after paying 6.2 percent out of their paychecks during a lifetime of work, they reach the required 40 credits needed for benefit eligibility—based on receiving one credit for every $1,130 earned, with a maximum of four credits per year.

This shows, by the way, that we would have to work for 10 years to reach the maximum number of credits, but we must wait until age 62 to begin receiving benefits.

Next we ask the Big Question: How much will we get?

If you reach Full Retirement Age—which is currently 66 (born from 1943-1954)—you would receive your Primary Insurance Amount, or PIA. To determine the amount you, personally, would receive during retirement, we at Reindel Retirement Solutions can help you come up with correct numbers.

If you have ever received a statement from the Social Security Administration that calculates, during your working years, the current *estimated* benefits you might receive, you can see that such numbers tend to change as we move forward toward retirement. As you get closer to retirement, all we need are your age, date of birth, your income and marital status to create a customized report showing your Social Security benefits. This report would be quite accurate, so you might take advantage of the offer.

Your Primary Insurance Amount from Social Security could be one of your prime sources of "green" money.

Social Security and Spousal Benefits

You might be one of those people who "held the fort" at home during a spouse's working years and had little or no earnings of your own to report to Social Security. If so, you would be eligible to receive income through the Social Security Administration "spousal benefits" program.

Here's how it works: You can file to receive half of your spouse's benefits once your spouse files to receive his/her benefits. Again, all the usual rules apply. If your spouse files before reaching Full Retirement Age, your benefits would be reduced accordingly.

It's important to note that two spouses earning high incomes can take advantage of the spousal benefits program. As one spouse files for benefits, the other spouse could file a claim for spousal benefits in order to wait until age 70 to file for his/her increased 130-percent benefit. In other words, when one spouse files at 66 with the other claiming spousal benefits, the one claiming spousal benefits would allow his/her personal benefit to grow.

At age 70, the latter would opt to forfeit spousal benefits and begin taking full benefits at the maximum amount allowed by the Social Security program.

This is just one of several ways to maximize your Social Security benefits. To gain a better understanding of the overall picture, we should focus on the five key elements of Social Security planning:

- **Now versus Later Benefits**
- **Spousal Planning Options**
- **The Impact of Working in Retirement**

- **Social Security Taxation**
- **Filling Your Income Gap**

When to Take Social Security Benefits and Why

By now, everyone should be asking the same questions.

First, when should we begin taking benefits? At first glance, it seems like the thing to do would be to wait until age 66 or 70 to begin taking benefits, in order to avoid a permanent reduction in benefits. Or, should we take it now and get less? We've already gone into a few reasons why people take early benefits, so the answer obviously depends on several factors.

When Social Security was originally set up under FDR, back in 1935, the Full Retirement Age, or the FRA, was 65. In fact, it is still 65 for people born before 1938, but as the years went on federal budgets and economies changed, and the FRA has crept up as well. If you were born between 1938 and 1960 your full retirement age would be determined by a sliding scale, putting your FRA somewhere between 65 and age 67—age 67 being the FRA for those born in or after 1960.

Again, we have the option of receiving Social Security benefits at age 62, but remember: You face an immediate reduction of benefits; again, wait until age 70 to receive significantly increased benefits, which will remain at the highest level available for the rest of your life.

Looking a bit more closely at the numbers, we see a variance of benefit amounts for every year you decide to delay receiving your monthly SSA checks. After age 62, for every year you decide to wait before taking benefits, you will increase your income by 6.25 percent! I've said it again because this is not common knowledge. It is most definitely something you should know when planning your retirement. If you call the Social Security Administration for answers, you may hear a lot of confusing information on the other end of the line, but this essentially is what they're talking about. After you reach your full retirement age, whatever that may be, for every year you delay taking benefits, your benefits will increase by 8 percent. That's an 8 percent increase per year, for every year you wait until age 70, and this will remain locked into your monthly check for life. In short, we're talking about big dollars over a span of years.

Begin taking benefits at age 63, assuming a $1,000 benefit at full retirement age, and you would receive $800 per month. Wait until age 67 and your median $1,000 income becomes $1,080, which becomes $1,160 at age 68, $1,240 at age 69 and $1,320 at age 70. These are *per month increases*.

Yet, we still see so many people going for benefits at age 62. Assuming the $1,000 a month payout at an FRA of 65, someone beginning benefits at 62 would get only $750 a month; they would see $800 at age 63, or 80 percent of full payments. The monthly check would amount to $867 when benefits start at age 64, and you would see $933 a month beginning at age 65. Poor health, a dire need for income and lack of probability for a long life include some of the reasons people take early retirement checks from Social Security. But again, I suspect rumors and emotion play a role in going early.

If you have other areas of income, let's spell it out: Let age 66 go by and wait until age 70. When you do, look at it like any other investment growing at 8 per cent per annum. That's 8 percent per year in the safest investment available. Along with your 8 percent increase per year, you will see ongoing adjustments for inflation, which vary, but we've seen highs above 14 percent in a single year (and as low as zero, but those occurred during an extraordinary period in our nation's history).

And, oh-by-the-way, you will receive preferential tax treatment.

Looking at the bigger picture and the $1,000 monthly benefit due to an individual at age 66, if she began taking benefits at age 62, the amount of total benefits she would accumulate by age 95 would be $306,000. By waiting until full retirement age at 66, her total accumulated benefits at age 95 would be *$350,000*. And if she waits until age 70 to take benefits, assuming she lives to age 95, her total accumulated benefits would amount to *$411,840*.

Let's consider a common model using an individual with other income. A male who takes his Social Security at age 66 and had a higher income during his working years is qualified for $2,200 per month. Let's say his portfolio also includes a $1,500 pay-out from his 401(k). Put the two together and he'll see an annual Adjusted Gross Income of $40,000 a year. Not too shabby.

Numbers will vary for each individual, so it becomes imperative to consult with a financial service professional to determine precisely where you will be in retirement.

Spousal Planning Options

Several issues may determine the nature of spousal planning and Social Security because married people have different options than single individuals.

When coordinating spousal benefits, first we must determine the exact amount of monthly income due to each spouse at various ages beyond 62. Most obvious, of course, is to look at the age difference of each spouse, then determine the PIA, or Primary Insurance Amount, of each spouse. Next we target the perceived age that each spouse would begin taking benefits, noting any health concerns in the mix.

As previously noted, we may draw benefits on one spouse's earnings, or the second spouse may share in the benefits of the other spouse. If you decide on the latter, know that you would face some extra paper work as there would be two income records to consider when tax time comes around, which could mean two separate tax filings.

Spousal Survivor Benefits

But here's a more important issue to consider: If one spouse dies before another, the surviving spouse would have the option to keep receiving benefits, or the survivor could switch over and start receiving the other spouse's benefit, whichever may be the greater of the two. This is a most unique and important benefit for married couples, giving each spouse a guaranteed income, which has historically increased by an average 2.8 percent per year.

While dealing with married couples, we also need to consider divorced or widowed individuals and Social Security income.

If a person was married for at least 10 years, went through a divorce and never remarried, this person might be qualify for spousal benefits based on the working years of an ex-spouse. Again, the same basic rules apply as to the age when taking benefits—you can still apply as early as age 62 and get a reduced payment. Two years after a divorce, you may still be able to receive Social Security benefits from the other spouse. You would be required to provide marriage records, which could also be located by the Social Security Administration.

Widowed individuals are able to obtain survivor benefits as early as age 60, again triggering benefit reductions unless the widow waits until full retirement age. Here, it's important to note that a widowed individual's Social Security benefit would equal 100 percent of the benefit due to a deceased spouse. If your deceased spouse had already been receiving benefits, the calculated benefit due to you would be based on 100 percent of the reduced amount still remaining, unless the spouse delayed taking benefits until age 70—which would give the surviving spouse 100 percent of the maximum amount of benefits.

If both spouses were receiving benefits at the time of one spouse's death, the surviving spouse would receive the highest benefit of the two.

File and Suspend

Once the Full Retirement Age is reached, you have other options often unknown to the general public. One of these is called "File and Suspend," which means that you can apply for 100 percent of your Primary Insurance Amount, but simply filing for your Social Security income does not mean that you are actually required to take your Social Security payment.

This strategy can come in handy for married couples. Here's how it works:

Consider the case of John and Laura, John being 66 while Laura is 64.

When John reaches his full retirement age at 66, he files for his full Social Security Benefit. Then he suspends his payments, putting them off for another day.

Once Laura reaches her full retirement age at 66, she files for a Spousal Benefit, which amounts to half of John's Primary Insurance Amount. Note that Laura has not yet filed for her own payments. Instead, she would receive half of the amount due to John. Meanwhile, John continues to let his PIA grow in value—remember, payments have been suspended—until he reaches age 70 and begins receiving payments.

When Laura reaches age 70, she can either choose to receive payment on her own maxed-out PIA or she can stick with the Spousal Benefit and receive half of John's amount.

Let's look at another scenario: If John's PIA is set at $2,200 if he takes payments at age 66, but instead he decides to File and Suspend his payments—let's say he has other income, in order to make this work—when Laura reaches her FRA two years later, she opts to file for Spousal Benefits, meaning she will receive half of the amount of John's benefit, or $1,100. Meanwhile, her own PIA is set at $1,000 per month, or $100 less than John's.

While enjoying half the amount of John's PIA ($1,100) her dormant PIA of $1,000 is allowed to sit and accumulate value at 8 percent per year, until she reaches age 70. Meanwhile, John reaches the age of 70 and begins to receive his PIA payment, but because he waited—due to his decision to File and Suspend—the amount of his PIA has grown from $2,200 to $2,900, which he will receive for the rest of his life.

Elsewhere in this book you have seen that the maximum Social Security benefit in 2012 was only $2,500. So, how does John come out with $2,900 a month? Because he decided to File and Suspend, the strategy allowed him to increase his monthly payment to precisely $2,904 for the rest of his life. At the same time, remember that Laura had been receiving half of John's amount under the Spousal Benefit, or $1,100. During that period, she allowed her own PIA to grow at 8 percent per year, meaning, at age 70, she can now begin to take payments from her own Social Security account, which now amount to $1,320 per month.

All told, this couple will now receive a total of $4,224 per month in Social Security payments. Had they both decided to begin taking their own, separate payments at age 66, they would have received a combined $3,200 from that point on, for the rest of their lives. Using the File and Suspend strategy, at age 70 they now get an additional sum of $1,024 per month.

File and Suspend is the way to go if, like John, you have additional monthly income.

Looking at the broad picture, the difference in total accumulation of funds is quite impressive. Add to that their ability to resist taking early payments at age 62. Had they taken this option, as a couple they would receive $682,000 by age 85.

Since John waited until age 66, and because he chose his File and Suspend option, and because Laura waited until 66 to take advantage of her Spousal Benefits option—receiving one half of John's amount—the couple together would accumulate *$882,000* by the age of 85. In other words, they would take in $200,000 more than other couples choosing early payments.

All of the above would happen because they took a brief, five-year period in their mid to late 60s to implement the File and Suspend/Spousal Benefit strategy.

Would this plan work for everyone? No, because some people must begin taking income at age 62 for various reasons previously discussed. But with advanced planning to create an income stream from other revenue sources, this plan can become reality *if you know it exists*.

Most people don't.

If you can look at this type of plan, we can take your own numbers into account and customize a similar strategy, wherein you might see $100,000 additional dollars at the end of the road, or more, or less. Bottom line, if you can make it work, you will BE smiling in the end.

Again, if you would like to see your own customized work-up for Spousal Planning, please contact my office so we can get the ball rolling.

CHAPTER TEN

Maximum Social Security Benefits, Minimal Tax

We've already discussed the difficulties of employment as we age. Now let's look at a few sobering facts: According to a recent survey by the American Association of Retired Persons (AARP), at least 88 percent of Baby Boomers plan to work during retirement, which sounds like a great idea, but this option might affect your net income in the form of taxation, among other considerations.

Given the devastating effects of recent economic developments on retirement portfolios—some lost 70 percent or more of their retirement savings in the crash of 2008—many people previously ready to retire have been forced back into the workplace. Yet, working might cause problems for people eligible for Social Security benefits. If you find yourself working between the age of 62 and you're Full Retirement Age, if you have been receiving *early* Social Security benefits, a portion of your benefit will be withheld if the government determines that you have been making too much money.

Yes, it's true, and too many people find out the hard way, so it's important to understand a concept involving the Lower Threshold and the Higher Threshold calculated against your total earnings as you receive Social Security payments.

Let's say your Full Retirement Age is 66, meaning you were born between Jan. 2, 1943 and Jan. 1, 1955 (according to the latest Social Security Administration statistics at this writing). If you find yourself working during your Lower Threshold years (age 62 to up to the year of your Full Retirement Age), as so many have and will, and if you are making more than $15,120 a year, the Social Security Administration will withhold $1 of your Social Security benefit for every $2 of earnings you pull in—again, for money earned in excess of $15,120 a year. Putting it another way, let's say you initially filed for your Social Security benefits at age 62 in January 2013, and your monthly payment was to be $600, or $7,200 year. Now, let's say you were still working and you earned a total of $20,800 a year. Your total earnings would have exceeded the $15,120 Social Security income limit to the tune of $5,680. In this case, the Social Security Administration would withhold a total of $2,840 in payments for that year, which equates to a withholding of $1 for every $2 you earned over the $15,120 limit.

The above represents the Lower Threshold of the Social Security limitation on earnings that would affect your benefit beginning at age 62.

The Higher Threshold begins within the year that you would reach the birthday of your Full Retirement Age. In 2013, for example, if you were to reach your Full Retirement Age at some point in that year, the Social Security Administration would take $1 of every $3 you earned—prior to your birthday in that year; this reduction in payments would apply to earnings in excess of $40,080. For example, if the birthday of your Full

Retirement Age were to occur November, 2013, and your earnings totaled $41,580 from January, 2013, through October, 2013, the government would withhold $500 based on the overage of $1,500—$41,580 minus 40,080—again based on $1 for every $3 you earned *up until the birthday month in which you reach your Full Retirement Age.*

Beginning with the month you reach your FRA, in this case November, 2013, you would have no limit *from that point forward* on the amount of money you earn. You can make as much money as you want, once you reach your FRA, and receive your full Social Security payments.

If you are self-employed, only your "net" earnings would count toward your Social Security income limit. Also, Social Security does not count the following toward income limits: earnings received from annuities, pensions, interest, investment earnings, and capital gains. Social Security DOES count employee contributions to retirement and pension plans IF such an amount is included as part of an employer's retirement wage.

(The information above can be found at www.ssa.gov/pubs/media/pdf/ EN-05-10069.pdf; for more information go to www.socialsecurity.gov or call 800-772-1213.)

Again, many people are unaware of this. They start working only to find their early-Social Security benefit reduced. This applies to your Lower Threshold period under Social Security Administration rules.

The picture improves as you age, once you reach the day you enter the Higher Threshold period.

Next, we'll take a look at Social Security Income and taxation, which has become a hot topic in recent years. As you might expect, I wonder where Social Security taxes and other taxes will go in the coming years. Congress will try to cover the deficit with more than a few items affecting taxpayers everywhere, to be sure. If it seems unfair to pay taxes on money we've all paid in through taxation over a lifetime, I'm with you 100 percent.

But it's a reality we all have to contend with. In the following section, we'll address taxation and rest assured, I have planning methods available to help alleviate the problems across the board when it comes to optimal Social Security planning for your retirement years.

Tax and Your Social Security

It is certainly an irony when you look at Social Security taxation and realize that we're being taxed for our Social Security payments, even though we put our own money into the fund through taxation. It's true: You will be taxed when you start receiving your Social Security benefits. You have already paid taxes for Social Security, and when you begin receiving Social Security checks, you will be taxed again, which seems like double jeopardy, but that's the way it is.

I'm not the only one talking about it. Lots of people are upset about the appearance of double-taxation in the Social Security system, especially when we were promised at one time that our Social Security payments would never be taxed. But the years went by and various government entities continually dipped into the robust Social Security fund, until it began to falter. New monies had to go in to replace the outflow. No wonder people who know history are really mystified about the plight of Social Security.

On the bright side, there are certain remedies available to help you mitigate the taxation of your Social Security payments, remedies that have been built into the law to ease the pain. You simply have to know what they are and how to put them to use, and I can help you. I have partnered with a team of excellent CPAs to make sure things are done properly. Together we can illustrate methods that would allow you to minimize taxes on your Social Security or even *eliminate* them completely!

Again, with proper planning, and depending upon your situation, we might be able to find a way to either *reduce or eliminate* the tax you currently pay on Social Security.

It all comes down to the amount of income you may be earning in retirement. If your income exceeds a certain threshold, your Social Security payments may be taxable. The method used by the government to tax benefits would focus on the amount of money coming to you through your retirement portfolio, which would involve the following: interest and dividends from various investments and accounts, and income from pensions and IRAs—in fact, they would apply these items after the interest you get from your supposedly "tax-free" municipal bonds and tax the interest you receive. (Always watch for anything claiming to be "tax-free;" read the fine print.)

As far as direct taxation of Social Security benefits, the government can tax up to 85 percent of what you receive each month, but it all depends on your income threshold. How do they come up with the amount you would have to pay?

Here's the Social Security *taxation* formula: They take the total income from all of your investments including bank interest, mutual funds, and bonds—*almost* everything you have in the form of income. Added to that equation would be any non-taxable interest you may receive. Then they add up half the money you receive from your Social Security payments. Adding these items together would determine your Threshold Income.

This represents your total annual income or those of your spouse if filing jointly, which may be subject to income tax. To expand the picture, if the total of your taxable pensions, wages, interest, dividends, and other taxable income along with any other tax-exempt interest income—plus half of your Social Security benefits—are more than a base amount, some of your benefits will be taxable. That's how it works, and for some people it could amount to a significant reduction of your Social Security benefits.

Another way to calculate your potential Social Security benefit tax is to take your modified Adjusted Gross Income and add that figure to half of the Social Security benefits you receive, or would receive, once you start taking benefits; from there your tax-exempt income would be added to the equation.

Here's the breakdown: Your benefits would be tax exempt if you were an individual showing an annual income of $25,000 or less. For married couples, the total annual income threshold is $32,000. From there, you would work from another set of figures.

Individuals with income between $25,000 and $34,000 may be required to pay income tax on up to 50 percent of their benefits. If an individual's income exceeds $34,000, up to 85 percent of his or her income may be taxable.

If the combined annual income for a married couple filing jointly runs between $32,000 and $44,000, then 50 percent of their Social Security payments would be taxable. If a married couple filing jointly receives more than $44,000 per year, 85 percent of the couple's Social Security benefits would be taxable.

Married couples filing separately would likely pay taxes on their Social Security benefits.

The tax information above comes from the Social Security Administration website at: www.socialsecurity.gov/planners/taxes.htm

Once again, you don't have to feel like a tax target when it comes to your Social Security. We have solutions and I'll share them with you in a moment.

First let's look at this situation another way: Income can take many forms, and it can be converted to other forms of assets. For example, you may have CD interest coming in that may not be all that critical to your monthly bottom line, yet the government would add it to your income tax threshold when calculating the level of your Social Security taxation. Along with other types of income, it could inch your total income into the 85 percent bracket. So, how many items like this extraneous CD interest do you have in your portfolio? This is one of many issues we might look at when taking a microscope to your Social Security planning strategy. I look at everything when it comes to maximizing your enjoyment in retirement. People are often surprised by what we can find. Some people have been amazed.

Social Security Tax Solutions

Here's a small example of solutions available to alleviate the tax by reducing your total income, which would put in you in a lower tax bracket: Did you know that a simple shift of strategy would put that CD interest into a form of tax deferral, which would eliminate this type of interest income from Line 8A on your income tax return? In some situations, adding this to other factors would allow your Social Security tax to *drop to zero*. Your take-home payment would increase, and due to my partnership with our expert team of CPAs, we would determine that kind of result, which would obviously work in your favor.

Basically there are two methods used to reduce your Social Security benefit taxation: one would simply reduce the amount of income you receive; the other would utilize alternative investment vehicles that would work differently with respect to the payment of interest and dividends. The obvious goal is to change the way interest, dividends, and other forms of income are counted toward your total annual income. My methods take all of the above and put them in different ways to maximize your Social Security payments.

We have methods and instruments available to accomplish this goal.

We can use Social Security tax-reduction strategies aimed at reducing the amount of income you receive. Then we reallocate your investments using instruments designed to reduce your Social Security taxes. These instruments have other advantages, but let's focus on the way they can make a positive difference related to your Social Security payments.

Our strategy is all about reducing your income—as it applies to Social Security taxation. Although it sounds like a simple solution at first glance, not everyone knows how to take advantage of this important strategy, which is part of an overall plan to change the way your investments work. Simply put, with my plan you would not be receiving dividends and interest *you do not intend to use* in the foreseeable future. Why wouldn't you be using the interest and dividends? With this type of strategy, we have certain types of products or investments that would help you maintain your income—in some cases even improve your income—while reducing the amount of threshold income you would ordinarily be required to report to the IRS.

This type of strategy is going to become increasingly important to retirees in the coming years and decades ahead because we now face an enormous national debt with creditors breathing down our necks from China and other countries. If we fail to reduce the national debt, all sorts of things could happen that would affect future economies, such as the inability to borrow more money to keep the country going. Because we face an urgent situation in terms of debt and deficit, our national leadership would most likely lean toward tapping entitlement programs like Social Security to help alleviate the problem.

If things continue on the current course, analysts feel that only 78 percent of our currently promised Social Security benefits would be available as of the year 2037. As heard through routine media reports, solutions to this growing dilemma include a "revision" of benefits and/or a tax hike, which could include the increased taxation of revised Social Security benefits, along with further increases of the official retirement age related to benefit eligibility. No, it hasn't happened yet, and we all hope it won't, but if it does don't worry:

I have methods available to neutralize the effects on you and your retirement lifestyle.

(Source of Social Security data/info courtesy of Social Security Administration/GPS Design unless otherwise noted)

CHAPTER ELEVEN

Filling the Income Gap and Factor "Y"

Part of the psychological fear surrounding retirement and the very entry into this phase of our lives would be one's removal from a bustling work environment, and the lack of a regular paycheck coming in on a regular basis. So many of us rely on that routine flow of income, which means more than just money, it provides genuine peace of mind because we know where our next meal and bill payments would be coming from.

Once that source of income is gone and, after further possible reductions in the current Social Security program, where would we be if suddenly the monthly Social Security check is no longer there for us? This has become a matter of increasing concern for several generations of Americans pondering retirement strategies in the New Normal.

Reindel Retirement Solutions

While these are the realities many of us face, there are genuine solutions available that would change or alter the way you look at retirement, and the way you implement new strategies—as opposed to sticking with shopworn traditional strategies, which appear to fall short for some people. In fact, without facing "The New Normal" in retirement planning, we stand to be left out in the cold if certain developments occur as projected.

So let's get started. Let's work on the "calm" before the "storm" and put your future in the right place.

First, you need a simple analysis to show how much you would need in retirement versus how much you currently have working for you. If you have done this in the past, as many have in one form or another, times have changed. Better economies have come and gone. It might be time for a retirement analysis "tune-up," and we specialize in that very thing.

I suggest this type of analysis as soon as possible, before you go into retirement lacking an estimate of what your actual situation may or may not be. Let us run the numbers to replace reality with speculation for you and your family. With that accomplished, you can start making accurate lifestyle and investment decisions.

The analysis may turn up what people in my business call the "**income gap**." Our job is to create a systematic diagnostic evaluation, so to speak, of your current retirement planning instruments. We also look at your current lifestyle and the kind of lifestyle you would experience in retirement. Then we implement every possible strategy to bring that life experience alive, either when you enter retirement, OR if you are already retired.

You may not realize the existence of certain options that would literally transform your current situation from one of living on the edge to a life far from the edge—with a safe, secure stream of guaranteed income.

We might utilize some of your existing IRA and/or 401(k) accounts to create the transformation. Additional resources may be found in your current brokerage accounts—all of which would fill your income gap to help you maintain a desirable retirement lifestyle.

The Color of Money

This is where we revisit our recurring theme—the "color of money"—which you would use to control investments and income that could become out-of-control (unless we can put on the brakes in certain areas).

As we study your current financial outlook, we determine the size of your income gap, if any. From there, we initially focus on the amount of "green" money you would need to fill the gap. As I say this, can you tell me exactly how much "green" money you would need to put in a product in order to produce your desired income in retirement? If you can't, I understand. The determination of green money—meaning "safe to proceed"—is often difficult for many astute investors to determine.

For example, one investment vehicle originally designed to give you green money in retirement was the 401(k) and at another time in our economic history, it did well in that role. As the economy surged, as if without an end in sight, investments placed into employer 401(k) plans served us well. But as we've seen through charts and other sources, market declines and other factors drastically affected the once untouchable 401(k). Working people started seeing unexpected declines in their 401(k)s around 2000 through 2003, for example, and it would happen again throughout the same decade. Then, from 2007 and beyond, the loss-momentum really began to accelerate through the crash of 2008-2009.

The other problem with the 401(k) is the limitation imposed by certain rules and regulations. We face a limit to the amount of money we can put into a 401(k) program, which may not be enough for a solid retirement. In fact, many a 401(k) has fallen short of providing a desirable retirement for people counting on this type of program.

Talk about shortcomings, I've had people walk into my office and talk about the way their 401(k) once had up to $500,000, only to watch it crumble during unstable markets and drop to $100,000, $75,000 or even below that point.

I could see that such declines occurred because their 401(k) programs were mired in risk. People in charge of managing the 401(k) were investing far too aggressively and the inevitable result of that kind of long-term strategy is—and will probably always be—eventual loss, even the occasional catastrophic loss.

If occasional panic is part of our human DNA, over-reaction makes up part of the picture as well. After huge losses, many an investor over-reacted circa the tech crash of 2000, putting remaining funds back into the market, into even more aggressive investments, in order to make up for a previous loss. Guess what? They would eventually lose again. This is how so many 401(k)s gradually eroded down to almost nothing between 2000 and 2010. It's a truly vicious cycle and it can happen again. It can happen anytime. Looking back at the so-called "fiscal cliff" debates in early 2013, dueling politicians could have triggered another recession, or at least another market drop—and the list of trigger mechanisms will continue to grow.

As a result, we now label 401(k) as being "red" money because it no longer provides the level of income guarantee most retirees must have in order to ensure a stable financial future.

This is why we first move in to fill the income gap with "green" money for your retirement. Defined pension plans, a.k.a. traditional "pensions," once provided green money as additional income for retirees. Unfortunately, defined pension plans have gone the way of the eight-track tape player. They no longer exist through most companies because they are just too expensive to maintain.

So, where does this leave us?

What if another type of product could enter the picture and save the day? What if it worked essentially like Social Security but without some of the obvious disadvantages mentioned earlier? Well, such products do exist and I'll present one here.

We'll call it "Factor Y."

Unlike a 401(k), Factor Y allows you to dump as much money as you want into the product. At the same time, it allows for similar roll-up increases of the type you would find in Social Security, such as Cost of Living Adjustments, only these can be built-in to Product Y in a way that would never change.

Far more important is the fact that Factor Y can nearly guarantee that you would receive a specific income during your retirement, indefinitely. Unlike Social Security for many people, Factor Y would be there as a legacy for your family when you pass away. In other words, as you use the value of

Factor Y to help support your retirement lifestyle, whatever value remains upon death would go to your heirs. Unlike Social Security.

Here it's important to note that the product carrier providing Factor Y must be chosen carefully by an experienced financial professional, who would select only top quality, sustainable products from top-rated companies well-entrenched in the industry for many years, companies with proven track records for stability and strength.

With that in mind, let's look at a Sample Client who opted to invest in Factor Y:

Mr. Sample initially started taking Social Security payments at the age of 62, which gave him a monthly Social Security benefit of $1,650. Other retirement income amounted to roughly $1,500 from a pension, which gave Mr. Sample a total monthly income of $3,150 per month.

In contrast, his desired monthly income at retirement was $5,000, leaving an "income gap" of $1,850.

In addition, Mr. Sample also had a 401(k) worth $387,887. It once had $500,000 but economic erosion took its toll. With $387,887 remaining in his 401(k), Mr. Sample was ready to put on the brakes, change his $387,887 into green money and create solid, sustainable retirement income for himself. He came to this decision after much consternation: Should he stay in the market and invest more aggressively to get his money back? Should he lick his wounds, count his losses and shore up his lifestyle with income guarantees?

Luckily, he chose the latter.

After careful consideration, I put the 401(k) money into a plan that would provide Mr. Sample and his wife with $1,850 per month. With this plan, if you put in $387,877 at age 62, you would receive $1,850 a month, which was perfect for bridging Mr. Sample's income gap. Once we had the plan in place, Mr. and Mrs. Sample had the $5,000 per month income stream they needed, and now it would be guaranteed. In fact, this particular plan allowed that if both spouses should pass away before the plan was fully paid out, any remaining money would go as a lump sum to a beneficiary.

Talk about a win-win scenario: To say they were pleased with the outcome is an understatement.

Green Money and the Income Gap

To put a solid retirement lifestyle into action, we must first determine the source of your green money. This is probably the most important aspect of planning for retirement in "The New Normal" since the Crash of 2008. We have to face facts and look to the future: Given global economic instability, increasing market uncertainty under a new trading paradigm, and the way financial service professionals have fundamentally changed retirement planning strategies, it is time to put "green" money to work and batten down the hatches.

At the same time, we want to ensure that your income gap has been bridged with effective instruments capable of creating a solid income stream—but only after you have determined the amount of green money you wish to have in retirement. Will it be enough? Will it be there when you need it? These are the kinds of questions I've been able to answer for many years, in the process saving retirement lifestyles from the ravages of time and shaky markets.

In this era, we definitely need downside protection and we need it now—before some other financial calamity comes along. If you are reading this and you are over the age of 50, even 45 for some people, you cannot afford yet another substantial hit on your investments. You absolutely cannot afford another hit once you have entered your retirement years.

For people in retirement, in particular, we want to emphasize the yield of your monthly income for your remaining retirement years. We want to take a close look and analyze every safe bet for your remaining nest egg as well, and if your choices include some active investment management, we can certainly do that.

In fact, once you determine your green money and put a safe, solid income in place, you can indeed continue with some level of market participation. We can definitely do that, even with instruments that would guarantee your principal while taking advantage of upside markets—*while avoiding downside risk.*

As an investment advisor, I can offer you an array of options with the bottom line secured around a steady income guarantee during your retirement years. I can actively manage your portfolio to accomplish a variety of your investment goals either before or after you retire.

Again, we must:

- **Determine Your Green Money**
- **Fill the Income Gap**
- **Protect Your Remaining Nest Egg with:**
    - *Active Management*
    - *Downside Protection*
    - *Emphasis on Yield/Cash Flow*

What We "Have to" Do vs. What We "Want to" Do

This is where we literally separate the seed from the chaff.

When entering retirement, even wealthy Americans must make certain choices. For the rest of us it's a mandatory process. This involves a process of delving into all the expenses we considered necessary during our working years versus those expenses we will need in retirement. Some people have been amazed at the difference. Clothing and cleaning bills once spent on work attire may no longer be a factor. Commuting costs and all the money going into work-related dining and lifestyles may no longer be a factor in your retirement plan. Those who worked from home would no longer need home-office expenses. We may no longer need more than one (or two) cars.

It's all about making decisions that would create your needed level of income. Before we embark on the creation of income scenarios, it is essential to explore different ways to fill the gap and put important plans in place for your future.

An important part of the process includes the provision of food and shelter, for you and for your family. These basic necessities formed the basis of what Social Security was to provide when the program began. Social Security was originally designed to provide the basic necessities in life. But most of us want more than that. We want to dine out and entertain. We want to travel and spend time with friends and family—all without fear of where our next income check will be coming from.

To make sure it all comes together, we want to take control of our red money and put it in just the right places, in green places to begin with, and in yellow investments if we decide we want managed assets on the side.

As you now know, you can take your chances: You don't have to learn about the color of your money, or plan for retirement, or fully understand how your Social Security benefits will work. You don't have to determine your base-line income. You can let it ride and just "see" what happens. But you should want to plan. You should want to determine your income early on. If you are near or in retirement, you should get excited about the process and dive in, because it won't take nearly as long as you think. Imagine that wonderful day when you'll be able to walk in the sunshine, knowing that the next day, and the day after that, will be worry free.

Some people never do this. They never know the joy of financial certainty. But you no longer have to live that way because you can begin your planning process right now. Please remember that the difference between a successful retirement and one ridden with angst is planning, and many people are surprised to discover just how much can be done with a little, but it all starts with you.

So far we've talked about the color of your money, the state of past economies and the relative "certainty of economic uncertainty" to come. We have looked at Social Security from top to bottom and we've explored some of the different ways to create extra income. We've also talked about when to begin taking your benefits and what to expect from taxation and the rest.

We've done all this because a startling percentage of Americans will one day depend solely on their Social Security checks in retirement, and I'm telling many of you now: Those checks may not be there as currently planned. They could be altered significantly at any time. This is why I like to look at every possible contingency.

If we get together now and start planning, I think you will be surprised at what you can achieve with the nest egg you have *right now*. So don't look back, look forward and give your chosen financial professional a call.

#

CHAPTER TWELVE

Who Ya' Gonna Call?

Now, let's consider one of the most important components of your retirement plan: I'm talking about the people who help you plan it (or not).

I'd like to break stride for a moment and talk about the people in my business.

The financial planning industry is full of good people who take a lot of pride in helping other people solve their financial troubles with the best tools available. I work with some of them because they specialize in certain areas of expertise I need for my clients from time to time. They call on me for the same reason. We help each other and our clients through mutual cooperation because we know it sometimes takes a team to make things happen in the best way possible.

Other people in our business are less inclined to provide solutions, more interested in making money, but that's life. It's up to you to make the best choice when finding the right financial professional for you. I can go on all day about changes needed in various aspects of financial services, although a lot of reform has been implemented since the great crash.

The real bottom line comes down to you. After reading this book, if you have some or all of the problems presented in this book, will you be willing to seek the advice of a qualified financial professional? I say this because countless people lost their retirements during the past 10 or 15 years, but not everyone can blame the rock-and-roll routine on Wall Street. Frankly, a good number of investors out there lost their shirts because they thought they could go it alone.

As if we've forgotten painful lessons from recent history, I still hear from people who indicate a strong desire to work with a professional, but in the end they still look for spotty advice from under-qualified friends and family members. I'm not blaming anyone. It's human nature to eavesdrop on a cocktail conversation when someone charismatic whispers something about a hot stock tip. This will never go away, and people will never stop suffering from the consequences.

The best way to avoid a fatal stumble into the trap of random speculation is to develop a checkpoint system. First, you listen politely. Then you check it out, of course. Finally, you run it by your qualified financial professional, your confidante with all the answers. Would this be a broker?

If you are in retirement, or over the age of 55 and still working, the answer is a flat "No."

By the time you feel the looming heat of your impending retirement years, you should be thinking about things other than risk. It's a difficult hurdle to cross for some people, but the previous chapters in this book have said it all on that score.

So, how do we make the transition?

Eight Ways to Avoid Starting Over in Retirement

- **I'd first suggest ways to say "No" to risk; say them to yourself more than anyone else.**
- **If an investment can be lost in a market drop, just say "No."**
- **If investments come wrapped in a package of "layered" risk, say "No."**
- **If an investment can't ensure a guaranteed income stream, walk away.**
- **If you find yourself scrambling to evaluate the value of an investment, run.**
- **If you hear about an investment, then toss and turn thinking about it, don't *even think* about it! *Fahgeddaboudit!***
- **If you are in or near retirement you need not think about risk in any form.**

You should be thinking about what you want to do in retirement, about ways to have fun for the rest of your life, and/or how much fun you can afford to have. Then set your sights accordingly.

If you hear otherwise from a financial service professional, you are with the wrong kind of professional.

Thus ends Lesson 1.

Pros and Cons: Lesson 2 Through 10

As I've said many times, there are many kinds of financial pros out there, many of whom are perfect for different stages in our lives. I'm the kind of financial planner you want to meet to plan the endgame of your years in market risk. You will never hear me suggest anything akin to gambling in the stock market.

If you have a company 401(k) and you are no longer with that company, why do you still have it? Are you aware of the risks involved with most 401(k) plans? In spite of catastrophic losses endured through 401(k)s during the great crash, this type of investment program may be appropriate for people young enough to risk the fundamentals of risk, which dictate that you can lose most or all of your money under a "perfect storm" of circumstances.

If you are reading this book, you are probably not in that situation. You should be in the risk-avoidance mode, which means you should be out of risk, out of your 401(k) and away from the managers assigned to manage that kind of risk.

About now, you should ask yourself: Who are these people, anyway? I'm talking about money managers charged with company 401(k) plans. Fact is, you probably don't know, and if they lose your money for you, I'm afraid you won't have the time to recover before retirement.

Managers managing 401(k)s are for other people, not you.

Thus ends Lesson 2.

Company-sponsored financial planners who come to your company talking about retirement can go either way. Some favor risk, some don't. If they do, don't listen. Politely get up, go away and find someone like myself. I'm grounded in years of experience helping people save every dime they still have. I will help you protect it and put it to work to maximize guaranteed income. If other planners do talk about guaranteed income in a favorable way, take a list of key points in this book and ask questions. If they're stuck for answers, if they tend to dote on one particular type of product, or if they argue about the necessity of multiple meetings to establish your retirement solution, you know what to do by now: do nothing; walk away and look for experience.

Thus ends Lesson 3.

You will find financial "professionals" in banks selling mutual funds, insurance policies, CDs and even questionable annuities being promoted by the bank—with few consumer-friendly features. First, you must know that these people seldom work for the bank directly. They either work for themselves or an outside company offering a specific type of product, while selling bank-related products for a commission. Chances are, if they have to sit in a bank lobby all day to recruit customers, they may just be starting out.

This type of individual might be okay for a young investor making his first foray into savings strategies. He may find himself in the bank lobby being talked into a variable annuity earning less than the average mutual fund but with the same level of risk, but he will have enough time to work things out before retirement looms.

You, on the other hand, need to walk into the bank, go to the teller, conduct your transaction, and leave.

People in your situation deserve, and must demand, a highly experienced financial professional to guide them through a complex maze of fixed income products that guarantee principle and, in my opinion, a share of the take from insurance company profits in the market (through fixed indexed annuities, etc.).

In short, at this point in your life you have no time for amateurs.

Thus ends Lesson 4.

If you run into someone who wants to mitigate your investment risk through the layering of securities among fixed income products, tell them you have a dentist appointment and get out of there. When people near retirement, the first thing out of good planner's mouth will be "income and principal guaranteed for life." When that has been accomplished, if you want to dabble in a bit of risk you can afford to lose, I can help you do that. But if a planner begins with terms like "asset diversity" and/or "asset allocation," you would rather be in a dentist's chair. It's easier to lose a tooth than to lose your retirement.

Thus ends Lesson 5.

Those still working sometimes hang on every word of the designated company advisor they see only once a year. This is the individual who hurries in, plops down your financial summary and hurries through an illustration of where you are, noting that it would take too long to go "into detail"—during that particular meeting—if you have more questions. These are the people who direct your questions and concerns to the incomprehensible company web site, which is fine for someone 20 years younger than you are. They can take a hit, you can't.

After decades of hard work you deserve your own, dedicated financial professional. Consider the way someone like me does business with someone like you: My clients expect a sit-down, face-to-face meeting whenever they want one. When they call, unless I'm on the phone with someone else, I'll pick up and talk to them. My clients hear from me more than once a year, with product updates, with account summaries, with anything else I might want to suggest. In short, through me, "they have people," not some bum's rush out the door after a five-minute annual "hello" from a company retirement counselor.

Thus ends Lesson 6.

Most people looking for an elevated level of financial guidance are either in or near retirement. Would that be you? Do you have money to protect? Are you thinking about how to maximize a lifetime income in retirement?

Sometimes someone looks great on the outside. They talk the walk and say the right things, but once your meetings have come and gone, you can't seem to contact anyone but an unknown "account manager" to answer your questions, even though you have given these people your hard-earned retirement savings.

In my opinion, you should never feel intimidated if you want answers to any question. As for advisors too busy to answer the phone, or call you back personally within a short amount of time, just say, "No." Find the advisor you deserve.

Thus ends Lesson 7.

Here's a financial planner most typically encountered: the one recommended by a friend or family member. You feel compelled to respect your friend's advice, even though you are not hearing things outlined in this book, including demonstrated experience with lifetime income products. If this sounds familiar, get a second opinion; your heart might get in the way of objectivity. Second, consider everything else in this chapter and base your decisions accordingly.

Thus ends Lesson 8.

Just as often, certain friends and family members might read the consumer finance magazines, along the way they probably cruise the financial blogs and love to talk about it. This is fine unless they think they know enough to help you spend your money (without genuine experience or appropriate licensing). This type of person will probably urge you to avoid paying "commissions" to financial professionals while steering you away from sound, professionally licensed and qualified financial guidance when you need it most. The best thing to do in this situation is to remember one thing: It's your money and your future; summarized information in consumer magazines might run in the right direction, friends and family members probably mean well, but none of the above are likely to know the complex world of annuities and life insurance policies. My advice: listen quietly and move on. Get with a professional who will protect you from risk and the likelihood of running out of money in retirement without a plan.

Thus ends Lesson 9.

Lesson 10:

If you can't find the right person based on everything you've learned in this chapter, call me. My contact information can be found at the end of this book.

Now that we've covered the bases from fixed indexed annuities, to the incorporation of the same with your Social Security payments, to the selection of an appropriate financial professional for your situation, it's time to think about how you want to pass it along, after you pass away.

This process can be fraught with unexpected twists and turns, and some estates have more complicated issues than others. If so, a properly experienced advisor will probably work with a team of elder law attorneys, tax experts and others best suited for certain parts of the process. I certainly do.

In the next chapter, we'll cover IRA beneficiaries, wills, trusts and other issues—otherwise known as the best way to ride into the sunset—leaving behind as little dust as possible while you are alive and enjoying your retirement—without having to worry about the following . . . so, let's talk about it now.

CHAPTER THIRTEEN

Beneficiaries, Trusts and Wills

The issues in this chapter come up when talking about retirement, so let's touch on a few key elements and follow with a few important caveats.

After working and saving for decades, you've finally made it. You've reached your chosen retirement age and if you are like many Americans, you have IRAs or other instruments not yet transformed into other retirement vehicles. If so, you may have a major windfall coming and subject to taxation when government-mandated, mandatory distributions begin.

While working, you probably set up things like IRAs, 401(k)s, defined benefit plans and/or other types of individual retirement plans, in order to defer taxation. But once you reach retirement age, your hard-bought savings become subject to distribution—mandatory distribution—and may trigger taxation, which many of us overlook. If you are one of those, you are certainly not alone. In my office, we help people in this situation every day and I can offer several solutions to put it all behind you, so that you can start enjoying your retirement with minimal hurdles from Uncle Sam.

It is important, however, to deal with pending distribution and potential tax burdens well in advance of important dates connected to your qualified plans. If you want to preserve and protect your assets and your retirement lifestyle from taking a major hit from taxation, we must sit down in advance of certain "trigger" points. We must come up with a comprehensive plan that will define a successful retirement for you and your loved ones. I did mention "loved ones," meaning family members or a surviving spouse because beneficiaries and legacies play into the comprehensive planning process at this point, as well.

First, we would fully examine your retirement needs. We want to identify things most important to you, which you would enjoy for the rest of your life in retirement. This means meeting all financial needs in retirement and the list can be fairly extensive for some people. Then, you should plan for the unexpected. If you die tomorrow or before you reach retirement age, have you included contingency plans for your beneficiaries? One of the worst things you can do is to ignore the latter and leave your surviving family members to probate, and the potential expenses and problems associated with probate. In the world of retirement planning this is like throwing your survivors under the proverbial bus.

If your assets are currently tied up in a company 401(k) plan, it's probably time to shift the money into an Individual Retirement Account, at the very least. I have other options that can be far more effective, but if you do nothing else, "roll over" your 401(k) retirement assets into an IRA. You can "roll-over" your retirement assets into an IRA when you reach retirement. Utilizing an IRA, if you die before reaching retirement, the named beneficiary of your IRA may be able to roll the assets into another IRA, or other instruments compatible with an individual retirement plan.

IRA beneficiaries typically include a child, spouse, charity or trust—which we'll address in this chapter.

That said, now it's time to deal with a most important issue: Required Minimum Distributions.

IRAs all carry minimum distribution requirements. Without following those requirements, your money would be vulnerable to hefty penalties. On a certain date—by April 1 in the calendar year following the day you retire or turn 70-1/2, whichever is later—you must begin taking distributions from your IRA. If you fail to take required distributions, you would be penalized with an excise tax of 50 percent of the difference between the amount actually distributed and the amount required for distribution. Distribution periods vary, but mostly occur over the life of the IRA owner, but distribution also can occur over the joint life expectancies of designated beneficiaries.

You will, however, find a glitch in the rulebook, which should be addressed as you near retirement. IRA distributions rules dealing with your assets—if you die *before* taking distributions—are *different* than rules that apply if distributions begin *after* you die.

In other words, it may be fairly easy to set up an IRA in the beginning, but things get complicated as you near your distribution age. This is where a financial advisor can help straighten things out. We deal with this sort of thing in my office every day, of course. We have all the latest rules at our command to make sure you keep current with the law, which can save you a great deal of money in the long run.

One of those rules has to do with leaving a spouse as your designated beneficiary. IRA regulations allow your surviving beneficiary to rollover assets into his or her IRA account tax-free. Or, your surviving beneficiary can treat your IRA as his/her own account without having to deal with distributions until April 1 of the calendar year after he or she turns 70-1/2, which means tax-deferred contributions can continue until required distributions begin, and this can be a distinct advantage for your surviving beneficiary.

By adopting your IRA as his or her own, the beneficiary can then name her own beneficiary and this allows a re-calculation of Required Minimum Distributions to include the joint life expectancies of both the surviving spouse and her named beneficiary. In short, taxes can be deferred for a long time if the IRA is handled correctly, although the amount of money for each payment may be reduced according to the joint life-expectancy tables.

This IRA planning strategy also has another name: In the industry we call it the "Stretch IRA." It stretches out the distribution period for a longer period of time in order to allow for an extended period of accumulation in the account, and if a spouse needs immediate income it can be taken through distributions from a rollover account—but distributions received before the age of 59-1/2 will trigger penalty taxation for early withdrawal and, of course, income tax.

To avoid penalty taxes, if you die it would be better for your spouse to receive distributions directly from your account. If you die before the age when distributions are required, your surviving spouse would be required to take minimum distributions calculated over her life expectancy beginning

on or after December 31, in the year following the calendar year of your death.
(*Data source: Gradient Investments, LLC*)

I'm passing this along to illustrate the need for someone who can monitor your assets, especially as you begin to enjoy your retirement. Who wants to deal with this sort of thing when you can be on a sailboat cruising the Caribbean? Maybe you do. Maybe you want to hover over your laptop night and day to keep up with everything. But if the latter is something you want to avoid, call someone like me because together we'll have even bigger fish to fry, like maximizing your Social Security, planning your guaranteed income and the rest.

In fact, I can think of better things to do with an IRA, but that's another story. Whatever you choose to do, make sure you understand the rules completely. If you leave an IRA to someone other than a spouse, this type of beneficiary must begin taking distributions on December 31 in the year following the year of your death but *no later than December 31st of the fifth year after the calendar year of your death.* Are we having fun yet? Probably not. Non-spousal distribution rules vary from spousal distributions, which differ from . . . . enough!

Would you agree that this sort of thing is better left to someone looking out for your beneficiary? In my opinion, it would indeed, if you want to enjoy life.

Again, without drowning in niggling details revolving around different types of qualified government savings programs, you need to have someone who loves thinking about arcane topics compelling as "multiple beneficiaries and segregated accounts"—which name several beneficiaries and money accordingly separated into different accounts to avoid, say, a future family brawl over Thanksgiving dinner.

(By the way, the oldest beneficiary in this situation sets the distribution period, among other technicalities spoiling future holiday fun if overlooked.)

IRAs naming a trust as beneficiary are dealt with in much the same manner, as if they were distributions from the trust to beneficiaries, which is great fun for a qualified trust officer to decipher. Not you, unless you are a trust officer with the appropriate legal expertise to sort it all out.

Then we come to a surviving spouse set up as a primary beneficiary while everyone else in the trust would be treated as a "secondary beneficiary," which could pose a variety of interesting interpersonal consequences if mishandled by an amateur. A surviving spouse could give up her claim to the IRA, or to part of the IRA, to fund a family trust in which all children were named as beneficiaries, which would provide the groundwork for distribution rules based on the age of the oldest beneficiary.

One benefit of trust planning is, of course, to allow IRA money to grow as long as possible without taxation, thus maximizing the compounding value of a growing pile of money as long as possible. The detriment of a trust is that it prevents the surviving spouse from making a tax-free roll-over of the IRA into an IRA, thereby commanding control of the whole wad of cash. Things like this can probably be seen in passing on TV shows like *Dallas*, but the Ewings always seem to have some intervening financial expert grappling with the devil in the details.

Either way, you don't have to be part of an oil-rich dynasty, like the Ewing clan, to have someone like me on board to handle your financial Rubik's Cube. It won't take long to set up the design of your own choosing, and we have the right people affiliated with Reindel Solutions to handle the devilish details. But again, the only onus on you is time. You must deal with all of the above as soon as possible. If your surviving spouse would rather roll over your own IRA proceeds into his or her IRA, without rousing excise and income taxes, this can be done with a *carefully drafted* trust. I said, "carefully drafted:" Online EZ Legal forms are great for lots of things—like getting rid of the bass boat your spouse hates riding in—but hiring a qualified trust specialist is the way to go when drafting a trust.

Why bring up trusts and IRAs?

This is just the sort of thing that can present itself when we juggle the different components of a solid, comprehensive plan for your retirement. I jumped into a few arm's length technicalities to help illustrate why it's so important to get it all done in advance, before you get into the relaxing swim of life in retirement. Are you willing to look back during that wonderful Caribbean cruise and try to remember when to start your IRA distributions? What fun to get a poolside phone call from trust beneficiaries squabbling over *whom* gets *what*.

At Reindel Solutions, you will have "people" ready to handle that sort of thing.

And it won't cost you a premium stateroom to get it done.

Wills and What They Really Do

Wills can work for you or against you, depending on what you want a will to do. Either way, a well drafted will can solve problems while a poorly written will—scrawled on a grocery bag by Uncle Fred—can cause major problems. Why? Because the mission of a will is to accurately convey the wishes of the deceased, in this case Uncle Fred. If it fails to do that, it winds up in the hands of a probate judge and the results can go in all sorts of different directions.

The advantage of a will allows you to clearly define who among friends and relatives will get your priceless collection of antique bottle caps. You might have a favorite nephew, a neighbor or someone at work who really stepped up to help you in times of need. You might want to leave something specific to a church or temple—such as a piece of property—and a will can define just that, if you want certain things to go to a specific charity.

Wills also tend to leave someone in charge after you pass away. This can become a sensitive task if selecting such an individual from among various family members (I wonder if this determined "who shot J.R.").

Regardless, your chosen "executor" will be the one who "executes" your wishes according to the written terms of your will, which explains why some families choose a professionally qualified individual outside the family to handle the job. The executor also can be an entity such as a law firm or corporation (ask a legal pro to explain), but in any case, someone with estate-management experience is a better choice than not, in my opinion.

It's important to choose carefully when selecting your executor because a considerable amount of money, and time, can be saved if your executor has broad enough powers to avoid continual petitions in probate in order to conduct an orderly distribution of items in the estate. This can be especially important if minor children and grandchildren are part of the picture for the lack of surviving parents, meaning successors must be named, or guardianship must be assigned, if inheritance becomes an issue. This can be addressed in the will, along with trusts created for the benefit of surviving minor children. With grandchildren, for example, you may want to relieve your survivors of the burden of asset management, as well as the complication of maintaining guardianship records and related expenses for accounting, etc., which can become quite expensive.

Real estate can be another issue, involving proceeds from rental properties under professional management. A related trust can be created and named in the will to assign assets flowing out of the rental property to designated beneficiaries, allowing the property to become fully available at a future date, if needed. In some cases, families opt to let rental proceeds or property values grow over a period of time, thus conserving the asset before distributions come out of the trust.

A "spendthrift" trust can be created in most states to keep a young heir from blowing your money on a proposed Ferrari factory on Fantasy Island, if college tuition and other prudent measures would be more to your liking. This type of trust could be set up to allow periodic distributions rather than the release of a one-time lump sum.

Most important, your will can designate a trustee to handle matters, rather than leaving your assets in the hands of the court, which may leave your estate to a court-appointed conservator and mounting fees for related services. If you do designate your own trustee, back-up trustees must also be named in case your first choice is unable to serve.

From there, a will can serve as a tool to make use of available marital deductions and maximize deductions for estate taxes.

In the event of an unexpected disaster, you can write in provisions for the dispersal of your property, which may become particularly important to a surviving spouse. A special provision may enable significant savings where a marital deduction would be involved. And your will can appoint assets you received from a previous will or trust to someone else, while additional provisions can assign responsibilities and interests in a business. This can be important if any previous agreements were made with business partners about business succession and the sale of your business. A proper will would clearly state your final intentions. The lack of clarity in this area can be costly to everyone concerned.

An executor can be named to either continue the business on behalf of the estate or to sell the business, if necessary. For that matter, your will could allow for the sale or dispersal of jointly owned property if you survive your joint partner, or if you and your partner die at the same time. Your will can even designate how state and federal taxes would be paid, and by whom.

If that isn't enough, here's one that came back to plague more than one family after the benefactor passed away: Without a will to establish your last confirmed state of residence, *more than one state could go after your family for death taxes* on, for example, the same piece of property. Lack of a well-established domicile can also cause problems in probate.

As a last appeal calling for the creation of a will, yours could deal with the continuance or disposal of insurance policies placed on the lives of people, the lack of which could become a nuisance as your survivors struggle to settle your estate.

So, a will can provide for many unforeseen situations that, left unattended, could leave your heirs in probate limbo for years to come.

When you design a comprehensive retirement package, the creation of a sound will can be a key component to your ultimate peace of mind.

A Primer on Trusts

At some point, if you really do your homework in setting up a comprehensive retirement plan, you will sit down with an estate attorney and discuss trusts and how they apply to you. Not all estates or retirement packages needs trusts, but given a recent barrage of ads, fliers and brochures calling for the establishment of trusts, I thought it best to clear the air.

First and foremost, you see lot of alarmist advertising stating a dire need for trusts. They would have us believe that everyone and his dog should have a trust, but a good bit of this kind of information is misleading or absolutely false.

I'm not trying to write the end-all definition of trusts. The subject is way too complex and I have yet to see any kind of layman-level document that fully covers the subject. Again, trusts are best left to qualified trust attorneys, but it always helps to have a bit of orientation. This will help when the time comes to ask questions as they relate to your family and the kinds of assets appropriate for a trust (or not).

If you have lingering questions after meeting with someone marketing trusts, always follow that time honored piece of advice: Get a second opinion. While trusts are a familiar part of what I do, I like to work with highly skilled professionals who *specialize* in trusts.

Now for a sampling from the basic language of trusts:

The general definition of a **trust** is a legal tool that will help people with their finances, without giving them full control over assets placed in the trust. Probably the most important piece of basic knowledge is that a trust may be either *revocable* or *irrevocable*, meaning the creator of the trust has the ability to dissolve or revoke the trust—or he doesn't. This becomes most important if the purpose of a trust is ever challenged, particularly when it comes to sheltering assets from things like federal gift and estate taxation.

People often ask me about the purpose of a **living trust,** also known as an Inter Vivos trust. This one is fairly unique among trusts in that it's created, also activated to work, while the trust draftor/creator is still alive. This is NOT a living will, by the way, which has to do with the removal of life support systems in certain situations. I'm talking about a "living trust" and the **settlor** of a living trust is the one who creates and often puts funds into the trust. The trust "settlor" also may be referred to as the living trust "grantor," meaning donor, which is important to understand as it relates to revocable and *irrevocable* grantor trusts.

Testators are those who act as executors of a will, whether or not a testamentary trust is part of the will; the **testamentary trust** is part of a will, in other words it's a trust created to become part of a will.

We all know this one: A **trustee** is a person who is trusted with the administration of the trust, but not a will. An "executor" deals with wills and the estate of the departed—whether or not a trust becomes part of a will. Yet, trustees and executors share a "fiduciary" responsibility, meaning they are legally responsible for properly managing property belonging to other people including a **beneficiary,** who benefits from items placed in a trust.

While a settlor and beneficiary sound like they may be one in the same, a settlor may not name himself as the beneficiary of a trust, and beneficiaries can include a settlor's friends, charities and others who stand to benefit in some way.

The **term** of a trust is a period time can be short or long, even lasting for generations if properly created, although most trusts are set up to last for the duration of a person's lifetime, possibly including the life of the settlor's surviving spouse and beyond. Terms of a trust often end when a settlor's children reach a certain age, while charitable trusts can go on indefinitely, or as long as funds last with distribution and management in place to keep them going.

We've already covered the basic function of a **spendthrift trust** but let me add that this type of trust also may be designed with creditor immunity. Such creditors may include state and federal governments, which can have far-reaching ramifications as you might imagine.

. . . Which brings us to Medicaid, a state-administered federal program designed to provide care in nursing homes and other types of long-term care facilities. Keep in mind that Medicaid was created primarily for the needy; understanding this fundamental principle helps when trying to comprehend why Medicaid case workers react to certain things the way they do—which may be unexpected and downright frustrating unless you know the ropes of Medicaid.

Medicaid rules include, for example, the spend-down of assets to poverty level before one can qualify for care. I have several products and strategies that come in handy when planning for Medicaid, which may or may not involve the use of trusts.

Why Use Trusts?

Trusts have traditionally been created for people who may be challenged when it comes to management of their own finances, also to handle funds meant to go to the needy. We often associate trusts with the protection of money meant to go to children and the disabled, who either cannot manage their own affairs and/or large amounts of money. Trusts also can be designed to help protect people from major creditors banging on the door. They can also shield a trustee's assets from supervision by courts, taxation and other issues, and a trustee is often directed to distribute assets from the trusts to other beneficiaries named in the trust.

The trust has been a popular tool among the dead for controlling assets they leave to the living through an appointed trustee. One example would be a husband who leaves money to his wife for the specific benefit of his children, although the trust is most commonly used as a tax shelter, to protect certain items including gifts and property from the IRS—after the death of the grantor/ settlor.

Trusts also come in especially handy if, for example, an estate would exceed federal estate and gift exemptions, exposing remaining funds to taxation, although gifts between spouses can have more exemptions than others.

Obviously, the use of trusts for tax purposes can be complex and tricky, indeed. A trust must be properly drafted even if both spouses are still living and ongoing rule changes require constant vigilance to ensure that trusts align with current government mandates. Either way, we're seeing a lot of hype surrounding trusts. High-pressure marketing companies may claim that "living trusts" have more tax benefits than testamentary trusts: To the contrary, at this writing the benefits are identical.

This is another area where a specialized retirement planning team can be invaluable. There are specific uses for both testamentary trusts and living trusts, which must be evaluated according to individual circumstances.

As long as the person executing a will (the testator) is alive and competent, a testamentary trust is revocable and can be modified at any time, although it turns into an irrevocable document once the testator dies. A living trust is revocable, more often than not, although some living trusts may be irrevocable. Life insurance trusts are normally irrevocable for tax reasons when initially drawn, for example, and a testamentary trust is essentially dormant until the death of its creator. Contrary to certain beliefs, the testator—the one who creates the will—remains in full control of her assets in her own name; she does not have to transfer her assets to a trust. As related to a revocable living trust, according to probate courts in the State of Connecticut as long as the trust settlor is alive and competent he maintains control of his assets. After transferring his assets to a trust and naming himself as trustee, he still controls the use of his assets.

So goes conventional wisdom that must—in every situation—be evaluated by a qualified legal expert specializing in trusts. In all cases, the proper forms must be executed with care and diligence. Asset transfers can, for example, become a burden and especially troublesome if done incorrectly because—if improperly executed—they may fail to be included in the trust.

Your legal professional would take particular care when placing real estate in a living trust, for example, ensuring that deeds are properly applied and, like any valid real estate transaction, recorded in a timely manner with required government agencies. To take back the land, so to speak, deeds must be appropriately re-conveyed, which may involve notification of a mortgage holder, a homeowner insurance company and all the rest.

Obviously, a real estate attorney should be consulted when dealing with properties and other assets intended for certain types of trusts, and so far I've never seen a standard "going rate" for their services. Fees generally depend on the size and nature of an estate, required legal documents and, of course, the time required to pull it all together.

The good news about the standard testamentary trust is that it stays as confidential as you wish until you die, when the will goes to probate. At that point, everything is exposed to public record, including taxation authorities, which doesn't sit well with most people, myself included. That kind of public exposure motivates most people to plan for retirement without being resorting to probate. If you've heard stories about living trusts being immune to scrutiny from beneficiaries, don't believe it; beneficiaries can petition the court for copies, along with accounting from the trustee.

Rumors also indicate that assets in a living trust can be protected from creditors, but exceptions exist, including revocable trusts used in an attempt to keep assets out of Medicaid spend-down. Rules may vary in your state regarding testamentary spendthrift trusts, if exactingly drafted, but again this is a complex, technical area of law and an absolute mine field of potential problems.

When we run into a retirement plan calling for trust work in my office, I call in some of the best people around. If you wind up paying a fee, you'll rest easy knowing the job will be done right the first time. And isn't that what it's all about? Nothing bothers me more than having to do over what should have been done right the first time. You should have the same attitude and be prepared to invest a little time, and comparatively very little money, to ensure that professional accuracy and knowledge are part of your retirement and legacy plan.

Do we care?

I've included this section on trusts because we hear about a lot of advertising and promotional hype surrounding trusts. People with little or no expertise come across with scare tactics, trying to sell trusts services to people who don't need them, and a lot of potential complications can result from the creation of frivolous trusts supposedly intended to protect assets.

I can often protect your assets from a whole host of problems without having to deal with trusts and probate. If we spot a situation that would definitely require a trust—and after consulting experienced associates with a high degree of integrity who deal with trusts every day—then we would go ahead and put it all together.

But I'll say it again, why go through the entangled web of documentation, along with extensive fees and administrative costs associated with trusts, when certain insurance products provide effective alternatives—along with guaranteed lifetime income, safe principal, an array of benefits for beneficiaries, and more.

Why endure potential problems sometimes associated with trusts including federal and state tax audits, lawsuits over trust stipulations, not to mention probate delays (often caused by inept trustees)—when it comes time to administrate and distribute trust assets? Nor do living trusts necessarily avoid probate in terms of applicable fees, estate and/or inheritance taxes (check your own state for more information).

Nowhere have we seen evidence supporting the notion that it's easier to attack a will, as opposed to a trust. If you want that kind of leverage, I have a solution: An annuity issued by an insurance company with a named beneficiary is another matter altogether. I can't think of another, more reliable instrument designed to protect your assets—as intended for your beneficiary.

I could go on, but I think we all know by now why so many people place assets in tax-advantaged lifetime income. With annuities and other life insurance products, you know where your monthly paycheck will be coming from for the rest of your life. You know that with proper planning, annuities can reliably provide your spouse and beneficiaries with your intended legacy, *while they avoid probate altogether.*

CHAPTER FOURTEEN

Empowering Women in the New Normal

For many readers out there, this could become one of the most important chapters in the book. It covers a key issue somewhat ignored at one time by traditional financial planners: Women tend to live longer than men and always have. As part of some of the world's wealthiest estates and corporations, women wind up owning immense holdings in real estate, stocks, bonds—you name it. The planning of their legacies will accordingly have an important effect on the future of this nation, particularly now and for millennia to come.

In the historic past, too many women left everything to the male-dominant role players of the family when it came to money. They were often left with less than what they had coming as a result. And in some cases, even today, a woman as a surviving spouse may be left holding the bag when it comes to neglected tax issues, after the death of her husband. This can happen if taxes were filed jointly while both spouses were alive and the list goes on: important assets were never properly transferred out of the husband's name; bank accounts lack paid-on-death stipulations or joint signatory status, leaving the money to the turmoil of probate; cars are improperly titled; surviving family members attack a deceased husband's will.

Are we forgetting something? Indeed, we are! Let's talk about women in the New Normal.

More and more women have become the primary breadwinners of the family—especially since the crash of 2008. Women are, in fact, rising through the ranks of labor and corporate America. They have been taking charge of their own finances for a long time. In many cases, I have seen them handle retirement planning better than their male counterparts, and with greater discipline and commitment.

As women continue to step into the workforce, taking high-ranking positions in powerful companies by leaps and bounds (although glass-ceiling issues still abound as well), women have become a major force in the investment world and in retirement planning. Many are independent, living alone, self-employed and often more interested in retirement planning for both spouses, more so than their male counterparts.

Let me summarize the retirement outcomes of two women covered in my last book, *We Survived the Crash*. Both are my clients and both reflect some of the many situations facing women and retirement planning.

One started and ran her own company, bringing her husband along with it until the highly profitable enterprise was finally sold. It was the woman in the duo who decided when to pull the plug and sell. It was the woman who got busy with retirement planning related to the sale. In the end, it was she who pulled together an array of somewhat disconnected resources and—after the sale of the business—put together a worry-free retirement, with enough guaranteed income for a very nice lifestyle in retirement.

The other woman brought the remaining assets of a deceased former spouse's questionable investments into a new marriage, grew them with her new husband and finally found herself faced with tough choices after the unexpected death of her second husband. He was a government pensioner. She saw the pension reduced upon his death. But she acted in time and met with me before the depth of the recession came along. Although she had to make hard choices in the beginning, together we pulled it all together and created, for her, a comfortable, dependable, independent lifestyle in retirement—and she's having the time of her life. She's also ecstatic about her own situation after watching her friends lose bundles of money in the recession. Back when, after announcing that she'd met with me and secured a lifetime of guaranteed income, some people criticized her move *because the market was thriving* at that point in time (as it is at this writing). Yet, she'd been there before; she'd lost money in the market. Ironically, as we prepared her retirement lifestyle in early 2008, the historic market crash was only months away. But again, my client had been around long enough to see fortunes plunge in markets past. She knew what could happen and it did. Due to her own past experience, *she* came through it all with a smile (more like a grin) and an easel along with paints and brushes. She loves painting. Rather than worry about where her money was going during the recession, she did lots of painting.

I have many women as clients with similar stories. Some are single, some are divorced or widowed, and some are married, notably handling portions or most retirement planning on behalf of both spouses. All told, they represent at least one important thing to me, and they say it loud and clear: Women command a massive amount of wealth in this country, and they will garner a greater share of the pie in the coming years. Women also tend to dive into the retirement planning process, some with even more commitment and discipline than men. They can be very meticulous about saving. They tend to put a lot of thought and care into their investments, so they also lean toward more reliable results—including solid income guarantees and guaranteed safety of principle.

I think some of this comes from a movement out of more traditional family roles. Although more educated and financially endowed than generations before them, women in the New Normal still seem to favor security versus risk more than men, some of whom tend to be gamblers until the day they retire (What am I saying? Some men still gamble their way through retirement in the market!)

Women may see "colors" in a different light

A wisely pronounced preference for security—versus risk—has had many women jumping into the annuity marketplace, but as we see a growing number of women take on the responsibility of family finances, they face an overwhelming array of options.

The options both in place and emerging every day for guaranteed income, alone, can be worrisome, especially when trying to plan a legacy for children and grandchildren. At the same time, I find that many of my female clients are becoming more confident about taking control of their own future. Today, they make important financial decisions more readily than in generations past. But they also tend to take the time for detailed explanations. Like men, they want to know what their entire retirement plan will look like when they get there and, as previously indicated, once they get the picture, they can become highly disciplined about saving.

Women are more scrutinizing

After dealing with a good many women as clients, I can safely say that they will scrutinize a financial professional more closely than a lot of men. They understand the value of my lengthy background in the insurance industry, and they respect my affiliations with extensively degreed experts in related fields. They also tend to look for higher levels of professionalism, so it has been helpful for me to have Registered Investment Advisor licensing with the Securities and Exchange Commission, along with certifications from the insurance industry and an academic background in mathematics.

Other advisors should be aware of this when talking to women. They can be extremely astute listeners and fact-finders, while being intuitive about people. When dealing with women, I learned early on to reveal more about myself and how we work in my office. My wife Janet and I work very closely in all matters on a daily basis, so women calling in to talk to me can visit with Janet as well, and—possibly as a result of having many women as clients—I think we maintain a more friendly and personable atmosphere, which can put people at ease while tackling tough issues closely tied to a woman's relationship with friends and family members.

In that regard, women seem to be more open about their relationships with others, I think, which can make it easier to gauge how to treat different beneficiaries. I also find it gratifying to work with women because my hard work often results in referrals to their family and friends.

In short, women may be more involved in the networking process, and they generally respect the expertise of others. I know it's a cliché, but we always joke about the way men will wander the countryside until they get hopelessly lost—only then relenting to ask directions. You find an immediate parallel in financial planning: Women statistically seek out the expertise of a financial advisor more readily than men. Women like to know where they're going from the beginning, rather than having to wait it out until the end—after years of traumatic market losses.

At the same time, women I've met in my office tend to be less over-confident about having enough money to last a lifetime in retirement. Together, we've spent a lot of time talking about what it means to be "comfortable" in retirement, less on a level of who will wind up with the most toys, more about how to achieve happiness and less heartache.

This is why women, more than men, will try to identify everything needed for a comprehensive retirement package from the beginning. It makes all the difference.

I've found ready acceptance among women for annuities. They're more likely to draw income from their annuities while men have a hard time moving funds out of risky market investments, even when they know the potential consequences.

In fact, I think something must rub off on married women as they watch their husbands tumble through the risk cycle. People in my business say that married women are more inclined to avoid financial risk, making them ideal clients. At Reindel Retirement Solutions, we're in the business of minimizing risk while ensuring steady income you cannot outlive. Women understand this. They respect the concept of "red" and "green" money. By nature of longevity of women over men, this is a very good thing.

Women, Longevity and Risk

Woman will live longer in retirement, hence the need for ways to make sure they won't outlive their retirement savings. Statistically, women outlive men by around six years. Practically speaking, I have seen wives outlast their husbands by many more years than that. As previously stated, women accordingly wind up with considerable fortunes as a result. In generations past, only then would they seek financial advice from a professional, but things have changed.

It's a different situation today. Forty years ago, most women would have begged ignorance about all things financial, including securities and other investments. Today, nearly half of all women queried from the Baby Boomer generation reported some knowledge of investing in securities while many reported extensive knowledge, this according to a policy brief regarding personal finances and lifetime income for women, a study conducted by the Wharton Financial Institutions Center. And those figures were obtained back in 2008.

Since then, I have seen a dramatic increase in women keenly, and independently, interested in the way the market operates.

Once they get on board, they show a lot of interest in preserving their workplace earnings for a secure income stream in retirement and, as a group, they clearly indicate a lack of confidence about having enough income for retirement. No wonder. Like millions of investors, many lost their retirements during the '08 market crash and economic meltdown. Around 2009, a wide range of women aged 65 and over, from singles to widows, relied on Social Security for at least 50 percent of their retirement income (this according to the Wharton study).

During the same time period, roughly 45 percent in the same group of unmarried women were relying on Social Security for 90 percent of their retirement income. In the final tally, pensions, Social Security and other forms of planned income proved inadequate to support comfortable lifestyles for unmarried women.

Having come through the crash and subsequent recession, more and more women are stepping up to do something about it. They favor guarantees over speculation. When asked if they would delve into risk with their retirement funds, nearly 70 percent of women interviewed in the Wharton study chose a strong preference for fixed annuities with higher lifetime income guarantees, while men preferred annuities with less income and higher potential earnings if markets perform well. The latter seem to favor equity indexed annuities versus fixed annuities and I have solutions for both sides of the coin.

Since the crash, many new products have been introduced that compromise higher fixed income guarantees with some level of earning participation if markets do well. But the differences between men and women continue, even if both are in annuities. Rule one: While men lean toward risk, women lean the other way.

But following generalizations and academic studies can be risky, too. This is why I always listen to the client and what the client wants. It's not about me, or how I view earnings versus income: As long as my clients understand the consequences of leveraging assets in market volatility for retirement, we're on the same page.

Their grandfathers would have been shocked to hear it, but as of five years ago, 26 percent of working wives were earning more than their husbands. I suspect the ratio has since grown in favor of women, who for several years have outnumbered men in the ranks of undergraduate and graduate schools around the country. It stands to reason that women will accordingly gain the upper hand as individuals in the workplace and as breadwinners in many more families in the years to come. If 95 percent of them now contribute to financial decisions among married people in the U.S., their voices will also grow as they continue to seek professional advice for retirement planning.

More than 50 percent of women already seek professional consulting before moving forward, which is the only decision to make, in my opinion, given the growing, mind-boggling array of products and features in fixed indexed annuities alone.

A Powerful New Movement

More financially astute than ever before, women born between 1946 and 1964—women of the Baby Boom generation—are said to be the most financially empowered generation of women in history. More women have become independently wealthy than ever before, while pursing successful careers and investment programs. They have achieved and learned more about successful investment strategies, while taking command of effective planning for inheritance from their parents or husbands.

This is why financial professionals have really begun to take notice. Since 2007, women over the age of 50 have come to own an astounding three-fourths of the nation's financial wealth, controlling a combined net worth of $19 trillion, according to the MassMutual Financial Group. And they are leading the charge with health and nutrition consciousness: Today's woman over 50 belongs to reportedly the healthiest, most active and wealthy generation of women in history.

Given the fact that they already outlive men by several years, no wonder women are more cautious and calculating when it comes to long-term income planning in retirement. They have to be! Through the next decade and beyond, women will own more than two-thirds of all U.S. consumer wealth. They will become the beneficiaries of probably the largest transfer of wealth this country has ever seen, with estimates ranging from $12 trillion to $40 trillion, as they stand to benefit from the double-inheritance factor: receiving inheritances from both parents and husbands (*this according to a study by Fleishman-Hillard New York's senior partner/director of new business development, Claire Behar*).

With this enormous transfer of wealth on the immediate horizon, let's remember the information revealed in this chapter. If current trends continue, women will introduce a new age of conservatism on Wall Street, and I think we, as a nation, will be better for it. Given this powerful movement, retirement strategies would trend in the logical direction of guaranteed income and principal.

From there, women with everything safely in place may come to us with more willingness to invest in the market, but I think those investments will be better founded in assets over sheer speculation. But again, that's my opinion.

As a company, Reindel Solutions long ago began catering to women, understanding the fundamental need to hear the voices of both spouses, loud and clear, before calculating the placement of retirement assets. Through the decades, we have watched women step into retirement with new confidence and clarity, knowing their futures are safely entrenched in financial guarantees rather than red-money hopes and dreams.

If women have been luxury consumers in the past, women as investors in the New Normal know what they can afford in retirement before they buy. Which brings us to an interesting point: According to Pam Danziger, president of Unity Marketing, mature luxury consumers place a higher priority on the *experience* of doing something, as opposed to the purchase of a *thing*. Running against what many of us might assume, women won't buy widgets simply to acquire more widgets, they want the widget to offer an experience to go with it.

The best annuities purchase and protect the life experience of the consumer. That's what annuities are all about. We don't just purchase stocks or bonds, hoping for the maximum return to buy more stocks and bonds. In the New Normal, discriminating women buy retirement plans to ultimately experience a carefree, quality lifestyle. They want the best possible features and earnings, as long as their income and principal will be safe from nagging market volatility. They also want quality products from top-rated insurance carriers, and they insist on hearing accurate answers from first-rate professionals who know their stuff.

At Reindel Solutions we've long recognized the power of women in the financial world, both those in control of enormous wealth and those stepping into careers while taking responsibility for retirement. Women step back and look for guarantees. Women aged 55 to 75 are getting away from the role of homemaker to look for financial security and convenience, and they find it in the plans we have to offer. According to Karen Vogel of The Women's Congress, women currently decide on roughly 95 percent of household decisions in or beyond their working years. It makes total sense to me that they would follow suit and decide how to secure a solid home-grounded lifestyle in retirement.

So, if you happen to be a woman still intimidated by financial decisions, don't be. Take a look at incoming trends and realize that women have a great sense of security and know how to keep it close to home. Women currently control around 27 percent of invest-able assets in the nation today, according to the Insured Retirement Institute, and the numbers are sure to grow over the next decade. This is due to the simple fact that 51 percent of women in the workplace are now entrenched in professional occupations or corporate/company management. From where I sit, if IRS analysts say half of all Americans with $500,000 or more in assets are currently women, they will have an enormous presence as Baby Boomers fill the ranks of retirees coast to coast. A decade-old study by *Women of Wealth* cited that more than 60 percent of women with at least $3 million in assets accumulated their fortunes on their own, or through a family business, corporation or professional career. Only 38.8 percent received that kind of money from inheritance.

Yet, two-thirds place a premium value on respect and trust. This is the most important factor to women when choosing a financial advisor. And this is why we have always made those values a priority at Reindel Solutions.

Times are always changing, but wealth has not always shifted so dramatically as times change. We are currently in one of the most electrifying transitional periods of wealth and power this nation has ever seen. The time has arrived when women are no longer excluded from consideration as chief executive in the White House; the possibilities are unlimited.

When I look at the fact that nearly 40 percent of the nation's top-wealthiest earners are women—and growing—I know they will change the nature of retirement standards in America, maybe even worldwide. With roughly 1.3 million women earning in excess of $100,000 a year, it creates a new level of demand for the insurance industry, and for myself. Yet, the qualities of trust and respect haven't always been traditions in the upper echelons of finance.

This is one of many reasons why we have been growing so quickly at Reindel Solutions. We have made trust and respect a reality through hard work and empathy, not just talk. We insist on many meetings before we do a thing for women as clients. They must be the ones to ultimately make decisions about their retirement plans. I also insist that my clients come directly to me with any questions they may have, no matter what time of year it may be.

Long ago, I saw the intimidation tactics of certain types of people in my industry and I walked away. I began to follow my own instincts, especially when it came to listening closely when wives, widows and working women began to speak. Lo and behold, I discovered just how influential their voices really were, when it came to implementing retirement solutions.

I'm not at all surprised that women represent the primary market for computers, financial and banking services, as well as automobiles and a range of other products. More recently, they have begun to outpace the growth rate of male investors in this country (according to The Spectron Group), and the number of wealthy women in the U.S. has recently grown by 68 percent, as the ranks of wealthy American men grew by nearly half that rate during the same study period, by only 36 percent.

As such, I felt compelled to devote this chapter to women, specifically, as investors, high-earners, shrewd and savvy consumers and probably the best when it comes to understanding the true value of my kind of retirement planning. I hope some of the research in this chapter has supported my position, thus encouraging anyone who might still feel intimidated about sitting down with a financial advisor.

As previously indicated, women are extremely important consumers. They lead the online marketplace as the consumer majority. As powerful net-workers, women are far more likely to share information about goods and services they appreciate, more so than men.

With that in mind, here's something I still find hard to believe: Even though women tend to be meticulous and detailed about their finances, often scrutinizing everything within a business/household budget, women remain misunderstood by certain financial service people—as if women aren't part of the fastest growing sector of investors in the country.

Many advisors in my business fail to recognize that women will earn, generate or inherit a massive amount of wealth in the coming decade. Will they sit up and take notice? Believe me, I have and when women speak, I listen . . . carefully.

Women have been coming to power in the business world, but people may not know that more than 75 percent of new businesses in this country are started by women. Not only do women make roughly 80 percent of consumer decisions nationwide, they now make nearly an equal percentage of decisions about how new products and services are made and dispersed—through businesses of their own.

Do I respect the value of a woman's business at Reindel Solutions? Let's just say that simple "respect" won't quite cover the subject: I have always seen the importance of women as clients; I now see women as a vital part of the *future* of my business *and* a major force in our nation's future.

I want women to know that when they walk into my office, they will immediately feel the genuine respect they deserve. From there, they will watch Janet and I work hard to earn their trust. I know it takes time to get to know someone in order to establish a high level of mutual trust. But that's what it's all about.

If you are a woman in search of optimal retirement solutions, I will help you through the process of finding income you can trust, income you cannot outlive, with a lifestyle upon which you can always depend.

So let's get started right now. The following are items geared toward married women BEFORE and AFTER the death of a spouse—many of which are things any woman can do to stay current with a retirement strategy.

(Sources in this section were compiled by David Reindel and Gradient Planning Services.)

CHAPTER FIFTEEN

How to Prepare for Everything: (Including the Death of a Spouse)

- **Always know where to locate important papers: Establish at least one Information Center**. While it's always best to keep everything in one place, some papers are so important they need to be located in a safe deposit box at a bank (a passport might be one such document).

If important papers are stored in more than one place—say, a *safe deposit box* and at *home*—put detailed information about the location of corresponding files on hand in both locations. Example: the home file should prominently *list important contact information* including the name of the bank and safe deposit box number, also the contents of the box. The safe deposit box at the bank should identify items stashed at home and what they contain as well.

If other documents are in the safe keeping of your financial advisors, lawyer and/or accountant, these people should be listed both at home and in the safe deposit box, along with their phone numbers and as much information as possible about items in their professional care.

If it sounds like a lot of work, it may be at first, but from then on you would only be updating your information periodically. I would establish *periodic days, once or twice a year, to update files*, which could be recorded as a reminder on computer calendars, I-phones and even on a hard-copy Day-Timer (if you still have one) to remind yourself when it's time to update your files, in all locations.

If you are married and some of your important documents are in your spouse's care, make it a point to ask him/her to identify exactly where they are and *what they are*. Again, write it down and store it in your home files and safe deposit box. This may take some doing, but both spouses must understand that in case of incapacity, or worse, others must be able to locate important information. This always requires knowing where key documents are stored, and where individuals are listed. *Insurance policies, medical powers of attorney, bank accounts, lawyers, tax professionals, tax returns, marriage certificates*, etc., should all be on the list. It is important for both spouses to recognize that thousands/millions of dollars, and countless hours and days, will be saved in the event of an unforeseen catastrophe.

And don't forget to maintain stored copies—or originals as necessary—of your family *medical records, trust and partnership papers, stocks, bonds, a current will* and the rest.

It's equally important for your information center to have a list of passwords for computers, online bank accounts and other places where your information may be stored.

Last and equally important: Make sure *a trusted third-party* knows where to find your information should you and your spouse die at the same time.

Single, divorced and widowed people should do the same, making sure a trusted third party can access your information if you suddenly pass away or become incapacitated. This is especially important if you live alone. It will ensure that your intended beneficiaries receive their due, also that portions of your estate will stay out of probate.

*   *   *

- **Know your Social Security!** I've listed this one separately because it can be so important: Within your information center you should also store complete information about your Social Security account. You want to have much more information than simply the amount of your monthly check at hand, including lump sum benefits that may be due for your spouse, or your children. Keep your Social Security documentation close at hand, for yourself and for your spouse.

This is where duplicate copies may be a good thing. While keeping copies of the last couple of years of tax returns for you and your spouse—which can be important for Social Security documentation—you should also have data related to your spouse's most recent employer and how much he or she earned, again for the last couple of years of employment. This is where marriage certificates for yourself/spouse and your children should be stored.

Similar to the way you record information in your information center, keep important contact information for your Social Security records, including the location of tax records, etc.

*   *   *

- **List and store an inventory of everything—physical and non-physical**. This can be very important in all sorts of situations, obviously for insurance purposes but for estate settlement and other issues as well. Art work and other collectibles including jewelry, electronics, guns, antiques, even power tools and family mementos should go on the list.

Non-physical items include legal documents, stock and bond certificates, contracts, partnerships, trust documents, everything and anything that would have an impact on legal proceedings should they occur. Insurance policies and annuities should be on the list as well, along with property deeds, mortgage papers—anything pertaining to your estate.

If this sounds like a duplication of the information center above, it is not. It's a laundry list of all things related to you and your estate. This list should be stored where you keep your documents.

In terms of *physical items*, you should take digital photos of your jewelry and other belongings. Make hard copy photos for your files and store the photos in your computer, should you want to fax them to an insurance adjuster, for example. Even non-physical items like passports can be photographed as well, as they may help in the process of replacing lost or stolen documents.

*   *   *

- **Review and update IRA, retirement accounts, 401(k)s and bank accounts.** This is where I come in. When it's time to take a look at these important documents, it could also be an excellent time to get together with your financial advisor. Together we can update beneficiary information, for example; I'll ensure that your information is updated properly. At the same time, we can review the performance of your retirement accounts to determine if your retirement plan needs adjustment.

As we age, we need to keep track of important dates having to do with IRA distributions, whether or not to begin taking Social Security for one or both spouses and anything else in need of attention. It might be time to modify the nature of your annuities to take advantage of the latest performance-enhancing features, while ensuring your guaranteed income stream and principal. You might think you have everything covered with a will, but wills don't necessarily guarantee that your assets will it make through probate and into the hands of your intended heirs. Only documented beneficiary designations can do that, and they are built into life insurance policies, annuity contracts and various other instruments. If you have assets at risk in a will, I would advise you accordingly.

Also know that bank CDs and bank accounts may be vulnerable to probate, as well as individual accounts with a brokerage. As previously mentioned in this book, these should be assigned to intended beneficiaries upon your death. Taking action right now will allow such assets to pass through probate for distribution, as designated by you not a court official.

*   *   *

- **Veteran benefits and government life insurance documents** should be carefully filed in your information center. If you, or your spouse, are military veterans, survivors may have benefits coming to them. As with anything financial, important dates and filing deadlines may apply, making it important to deal with these documents as soon as possible.

*   *   *

-   **Records of all debt** should be kept handy, maybe in a separate file as this kind of debt is in constant flux. Credit card debt, lines of credit, mortgage debt, auto loans and the rest should be available and easy to locate.

*   *   *

-   **Powers of attorney, wills, trusts and guardianships** can be important and they should be kept with all other important documents in your information center. You can see why guardianship documents could be vital for the welfare of minor children, for example. They must be kept wherever your important documents are stored.

*   *   *

-   **If you haven't chosen a professional financial advisor, do so.** Most people take care of this one before retirement, but if it's still on your to-do list, make sure your advisor is a "retirement" advisor. This means he or she will be most interested in preserving your well-being in retirement, which does not include market volatility and risk. Your advisor-of-choice should demonstrate a thorough expertise with annuities and related insurance products. A good advisor will tell you during the first meeting that more meetings and your financial and personal information will be necessary before a comprehensive plan can be put in place for you.

Your financial advisor can also guide you when it comes to any additional expertise you may need (tax/legal, etc.). And the right advisor will assure that he or she will be personally available to meet or speak with you throughout the year, should you have anything in mind that would keep you awake at night.

As I said before, it takes trust and respect on both sides of the desk to make for a good match between a client and advisor. If it doesn't feel right, try again, get a second opinion, but find yourself a trusted advisor before you do anything else. A good advisor can be more valuable than a best friend during a family crisis, while keeping your retirement on track no matter what happens in the market.

*   *   *

- **Choosing an estate administrator.** Once you have gone through all of the above, when you have an advisor in place and all your inventories and documents are in place, you will need an estate administrator willing to follow your directives and distribute your assets after you die. Would this be a close friend or spouse? Not necessarily either, because they may be too emotionally devastated to deal with the burden when it really counts.

Either way, once you have chosen your estate administrator, this individual should receive copies of your estate planning documents as soon as possible. Contact information for your estate administrator should be prominently listed in your information center.

*   *   *

- Finally, your **burial plan** and funeral event pre-planning should be discussed with your spouse and/or appropriate family members or friends. A burial policy can be a good thing to have, but sometimes they act like insurance policies and should be treated accordingly. Your advisor may be able to help you in this area, or he/she can direct you to reliable people in the end-of-life industry.

*   *   *

THINGS TO DO *AFTER* THE DEATH OF A SPOUSE:
(Single and divorced people can use much of this information as well.)

The following would, of course, come after family gatherings and memorial events—after the first, emotionally difficult times have passed and healing has begun. But don't wait *too long* to deal with important issues surrounding your estate. After all, everything discussed in the list above has been in preparation for your action below. Because things in the financial and legal world move quickly after a death, it is important to get started right away.

- Based on groundwork already covered above, now it's time to **assemble the records from your information center**. Included in your consolidated package of information would be keys to safe deposit boxes, codes and passwords, everything someone might need to help you through the post-end-of-life process. Since you (should) already have everything in order in terms of financial and legal documentation, you're ready for the next step.

*   *   *

- **Contact your financial advisor.** Following the death of a spouse and the emotional moments to follow, it will be hard to think about things like money and property. This is the time to meet with your financial advisor to ensure that *your* legacy goes to the right people. If you should die suddenly, or become incapacitated, who would designate your heirs as the rightful recipients of your assets? In short, don't pass up opportunities to put everything in place as you deal with other issues.

*   *   *

- **Update your beneficiary information.** This item goes with the meeting you should have with your financial advisor. After the death of your spouse, all sorts of benefits come alive for your beneficiaries and important documents and events must be filed to get the ball rolling. Given all of the information you have already assembled, your financial advisor should be able to take it from this point forward, but your participation will be necessary through the process.

*   *   *

- **Time to talk about the future.** You have done everything possible at a difficult time to let the right people settle matters of your estate. Your documents were ready—without your having to think too much about them—your team of professionals and the estate administrator were listed in your information center. Now it's time for one of the most difficult moments for many of us: It's time to pull the immediate family together and talk about *your wishes*, about any directions you would put in place if your health were in jeopardy, or if you were involved in an accident that might *not* lead to your death.

Maybe it's also time to talk about the future of assets left behind by your spouse, as they relate to your plans for the estate. This would be a good time to introduce the name of your financial advisor, should any beneficiaries need help with newly acquired assets.

*   *   *

- **List people to be contacted if you die.** The list of people to be contacted should already be in your information center. You could make a separate list and pass it along to family members or friends, so they will know whom to notify in case you pass away.

*   *   *

- **Never travel without important information**. It is not uncommon for people to leave home after a death in the family. You might take a vacation or visit friends and relatives. Whenever traveling away from home, assemble a list of important information to take with you. Identify prescription medicines, people to contact in case of emergency, health insurance providers and more. Some people even code the contact and account numbers for credit cards and bank accounts, in case cards are lost or stolen. Also, it's always a good idea to know where your health provider's nearest facility is located.

*   *   *

TAKING CHARGE

As I wind up this all-too-brief summary about planning for retirement, I'd like to add that most of the basics apply to everyone—female, male, single, divorced, whomever.

In retirement, we should detoxify the risk-volatility in our retirement plans. We should be thinking about income guarantees that will last a lifetime. The last thing on our minds should be the risk of principal.

Meanwhile, we haven't talked about long-term care or specialized financial services for people with large estates and extended families, but wealth management is part of what I do. I can help with virtually anything you and your family need to lock-down a solid future, as you live out carefree days in your retirement.

CHAPTER SIXTEEN

Long-Term Care and Your Survivors

No comprehensive retirement plan would cover everything without looking at the soaring costs of long-term care. After maximizing your Social Security benefits and securing a stream of guaranteed income, you should protect yourself from financial setbacks due to unexpected long-term care in a nursing home.

Catastrophic illness and debilitating accidents in the home can strike without warning. Such events can devastate the best-laid plans for retirement, but here's the good news: Options are available to avoid significant financial loss if you encounter the unexpected.

Unfortunately the likelihood of suffering a catastrophic illness or accident becomes more common as we age. This is why you should start planning now.

You may be in the pink of health today and according to the latest data people in America seem to be living longer than ever before. Back in 1947, the average man lived from 45 to 50 years. Today, American men can live well into their 90s, so reaching the retirement age of 65 is hardly much of a feat these days—in fact, it could be said that "today's 70 is the new 45"—in the New Normal. Which sounds fantastic until we consider a sobering reality: The longer we live the more likely we'll need some form of long-term care in a nursing home.

Medical advances have led to miraculous cures and treatments for heart disease, cancer, stroke and kidney disease—one of two people in the U.S. will be diagnosed with some kind of cancer in their lifetime although cure-rates are increasing for many types of cancer. (Source: Centers for Disease Control) Yet, we still face conditions like Parkinson's and Alzheimer's. More than 40 percent of Americans over 85 have some form of Alzheimer's and dementia's still out there, *along with non-fatal maladies* that put people in nursing homes for extended periods. Crippling bone breaks, severe arthritis and other issues may lead to nursing home confinement for months or even years—all of which leads to a sobering fact: According to the Health Care Financial Association, if you take a group photo of seniors today, roughly half of those in the picture will wind up in a nursing home.

Do we panic? Of course not. We plan.

We all know the realities of Medicare funding under Obama Care. With or without Obama Care, the writing was on the wall anyway: Soaring hospital fees and the rising cost of prescription drugs will put seniors living on fixed incomes in a growing financial squeeze. Health insurance benefits have been steadily decreasing with premiums increasing due to age and other factors. Yet, many of those costs still fall under Medicare coverage until a hospitalized/institutionalized patient requires care for more than 100 days (go to the federal Medicare website for more information, or call my office for a more detailed illustration of long-term care today).

And here's a reality we often overlook: Many people *do get better* in nursing homes, but after a few years of care they may go home penniless without planning.

While most stroke victims live through the first event, more than 60 percent may require some form of long-term care. Kidney failure and heart disease also may require treatment programs demanding extended periods of long-term care. After that, after retirement savings have been unexpectedly depleted for lack of planning, people may be released without assets because too many assume that the government will pick up the tab.

When many people think of long-term care we assume we'll be covered under Medicaid. This could be one of the most expensive mistakes you'll ever make. Medicaid is a dicey prospect unless you are prepared to become impoverished down to bare-bones assets. Medicaid caseworkers investigate every asset you have from bank accounts and investments to cars, gold, whatever. Meanwhile, you'll be paying for your extended nursing home out of pocket until Medicaid coverage kicks in, which would happen if the assets above are counted, included in items marked for "spend-down" and liquidated for nursing home costs. Only then would Medicaid pick up the tab for your nursing home care, unless you take measures to avoid spend-down.

Without planning, if you, or your spouse, are hit by any number of illnesses deemed "catastrophic" in health-care vernacular, you may wind up shelling out $6,000 to $10,000 *per month* for a bed in a nursing home. Again, Medicaid equations can be complicated but the truth is simple: Medicaid spend-down isn't the way you want to go if you can avoid it, and, *yes, you can avoid it.*

It all comes down to alleviating or eliminating the value of "financial snapshots" taken by Medicaid caseworkers looking backward in time. They look at "snapshots" of every last nickel you've spent during a five-year "look-back" period, which begins the day you apply for Medicaid. Let's assume for now that everything including money gifted to your children, college tuition for grandchildren, Social Security checks, pensions, IRA distributions and investment income—and more, in fact just about everything—can indeed count for spend-down. They may tally up everything and if it all comes to, say, $200,000, you would have to pay in $200,000 for your long-term care in a nursing home before Medicaid would pay a dime. (To complicate matters, Medicaid rules vary state-by-state.)

With nursing home fees coming in at around $80,000 a year, it won't take long to rack up $200,000 in fees.

Again, I've said it more than once and I'll say it again: Medicaid variables abound. Get professional help if you think you have potential spend-down issues. Better yet, you should contact a professional advisor like myself and learn how to avoid spend-down altogether. I can help. Unless you want to wind up being one of the hapless 23 percent of patients paying 100 percent out of pocket for their nursing home care, let's explore your options immediately—before the unexpected strikes.

One option is long-term care insurance. Of course, we've all heard about the high cost of long-term care insurance, but even at the highest levels, premiums can be less expensive than the alternative—the potential decimation of your retirement savings. Yet, working together we can reduce the cost of long-term care coverage. For example, some people tackle the five-year look-back period with the purchase of a five-year, long-term care policy to cover the Medicaid look-back period. From Day One in a nursing home the patient uses the insurance policy to cover nursing home care for the next five years. During that period, assets can be gifted and transferred until the five-year look-back period expires. If you are still under nursing home care at that point, the look-back period begins again and Medicaid would pick up the tab because you would have no remaining assets. Again, get expert help in this area as Medicaid rules vary.

If you have a long term care policy that qualifies for tax deductions, the Kennedy-Kassel Baum Act of 1966 allows the deduction of nursing home premiums, but here you need the expert assistance of a qualified tax professional, whom you will find through my office if need be. Rules change and we're in the business of keeping up with them, while maintaining a close eye on all of the latest long-term care products out there. We can help you calculate the amount of coverage you need but I heartily suggest getting started before you find yourself on the wrong side of the nursing home equation. Long-term care costs are the only wild card in guaranteed retirement planning because things happen out of the blue, without warning.

You might have heard that certain annuities can be used in Medicaid planning. It's true in some states but you must proceed with caution. Not all annuities are Medicaid compliant in all states. Medicaid compliant annuities must follow exacting guidelines provided by each individual state. As such, only a few carriers offer Medicaid compliant annuities, but they're out there.

Providing for a Surviving Spouse

It's a different story when creating strategies for survivors.

In this book we have covered ways for Social Security checks to be increased for a surviving spouse. Annuities and pensions can be modified to ensure monthly income for your spouse if you pass away, and by now you know how your survivor can be affected without some alteration of your investment vehicles.

When it's time to create reliable, guaranteed income, I have shown you how to ensure that your spouse will have income after you die and that related taxes will be minimal, if any.

Again, women sometimes express a preference for traditional fixed annuities because they may appear to offer slightly higher, fixed interest rates without variation. However, it's important to remember that fixed *indexed* annuities can create an income stream while protecting your guaranteed principal. They also ensure that every gain you make will be protected after an up-market declines, *and*, like the traditional fixed annuity, they can provide a base amount of fixed interest every year.

Whatever your needs may be, it's all about making a decision to sit down with a qualified advisor. Together we will put a plan in place to provide for you and your survivors, whoever they may be. You and your spouse would come away with a crystal clear picture of the outcome, should one, or both of you, pass away.

By now you know why this is so important. You know what can happen without planning: The surviving spouse stands to suffer a serious drop in income; pensions evaporate. This was especially rampant when traditional pensions ruled the world because many pensions were structured to end upon the pensioner's death, leaving the survivor with little more than a reduced check from Social Security. Families were often burdened unnecessarily when that happened because an elderly mom or dad were forced to move in with a younger generation, and the newly bereaved widow/widower accordingly lost his or her financial independence in the process.

None of the above need happen in the New Normal.

New Normal Solutions

While traditional pensions have largely become a thing of the past, a new generation of pension-like instruments act like pensions with more features, death benefits and even long-term care provisions, all of which can be designed to fit your own, individual retirement needs. Again, it's all about putting the rubber to road when it comes to retirement planning.

Make Your Money Last a Lifetime

You should know enough about me to know that I'm all about asset preservation, as opposed to market volatility.

Asset planning in my book (this one, in fact) is focused on the ability to make your money last as long as you and your surviving spouse may live.

The next issue revolves around the way you want to live and that drives the real question: When do you want to **a.)** Sit down with me and **b.)** Come up with a plan in order to **c.)** Commit to a retirement lifestyle you can count on *for as long as you live?*

It can begin with a lump sum contribution or an energized new plan to set aside more money—money earmarked for income and principal guaranteed. And I have an excellent choice of lifetime income alternatives waiting in my office, which sometimes trigger a surprising response. With some of these instruments you may be able to retire right now and not even know it! All we have to do is sit down and analyze your current qualified plans. The combined power of your 401(k) and IRAs might, for example, have more value than you think when added to Social Security and other assets.

I'm saying that you might find yourself looking at a more immediate exit-strategy from work than you ever dreamed possible. But you may never know unless we get together.

Retire Safe and Financially Sound

Wherever you may be retirement-wise, the New Normal is no longer tied to relentless risk-taking in markets destined to offer dizzying gains followed by sobering declines. I hope we never see another Great Recession. Hopefully, enough people nearing retirement have gotten wise to Wall Street cycles. Hopefully, more people in this age group are ready to go with lifetime guarantees instead of risk. In my opinion, this would help ease the effects of another crash. I'm not alone in this way of thinking.

Many people in my business have learned hard lessons since 2008. A number of those who once specialized solely in market investments have come around, offering at least a New Normal foundation in guaranteed income.

As I've said throughout this book, after you establish a lifetime income and if you want to speculate bit, I can help you with that through a team of specialists. Just know that we're all driven to protect you and your financial security for the rest of your life, and that's the bottom line.

Forget Fiscal Cliffs. Let someone else worry about upheaval in the Spanish/Greek/Whatever stock exchange. Who needs it?

Consolidate, reallocate. Make your best move now and negative future economies will be little more than distant headlines. With my comprehensive brand of planning, you will simply go on with your life and enjoy it to the fullest.

#

MY PARTING NOTE TO YOU

. . . Thank You and Best Wishes

I know how valuable your time truly is, so let me thank you sincerely for taking the time to read this book.

If nothing else, I hope I've been able to present new concepts that will change the way you look at retirement planning. Some of you may be in the earlier phase of your earning years. Others may be in retirement or preparing for the big day when work is all about planning your next vacation.

What am I saying? In retirement you're supposed to be on vacation every day!

I'm here to keep it that way, and now you know what to look for when looking for a financial advisor. It may be me. It may be someone on the other side of the world. Either way, I hope you will consider the messages presented here because I see absolutely no reason *whatsoever* for anyone to worry about going broke in retirement.

I'm happy to say that we are now living in a remarkable New Normal of retirement planning. Tools exists today that were unheard of only a few years ago. Insurance carriers are far more consumer friendly today than they were in the past, and customers are far more savvy than ever before when it comes to retirement planning.

All told, conditions in the New Normal since the crash of 2008 have made my job even more enjoyable. I love nothing more than to see a big smile on a client's face when they realize that retirement is not only possible, it's close enough to reach out and touch.

That's why I truly love what I do, and I can do the same for you. For now, best wishes, take heart and know that we're here for you all the way.

Sincerely,
David Reindel

1 Allen Street
Mystic, CT 06355
800-639-5113
860-245-0633
reindel@comcast.net

CPSIA information can be obtained at www.ICGtesting.com
Printed in the USA
BVOW08s0156170913

331324BV00001B/1/P